BOULDERING
Movement, Tactics, and Problem Solving

MOUNTAINEERS
OUTDOOR EXPERT
series

BOULDERING
Movement, Tactics, and Problem Solving

Peter Beal

Foreword by Dave Graham

THE MOUNTAINEERS BOOKS

THE MOUNTAINEERS BOOKS
is the nonprofit publishing arm of The Mountaineers, an organization founded in 1906 and dedicated to the exploration, preservation, and enjoyment of outdoor and wilderness areas.

1001 SW Klickitat Way, Suite 201, Seattle, WA 98134

First edition, 2011

Distributed in the United Kingdom by Cordee, www.cordee.co.uk

Manufactured in the United States of America

Copy Editor: Erin Moore
Cover and Book Design: The Mountaineers Books
Layout: Jennifer Shontz, Red Shoe Design
All photographs by author unless otherwise noted.
Cover photograph: *Cody Roth finds a creative stem in Baja, Mexico.* (Photo by Andrew Burr)
Back cover photograph: *Colette McInerney heelhooking and crimping on* Animal Acts *(V5), Hueco Tanks* (Photo by Caroline Treadway)
Frontispiece: *Josh Fowler bouldering near Little River Canyon in Fort Payne, Alabama* (Photo by Andrew Kornylak)

Library of Congress Cataloging-in-Publication Data

Beal, Peter, 1964–
 Bouldering : movement, tactics, and problem solving / by Peter Beal.
   p.   cm.
 Includes bibliographical references.
 ISBN 978-1-59485-500-9 (pbk.) — ISBN 978-1-59485-501-6 (ebook)
1. Rock climbing. I. Title.
 GV200.2.B43 2011
 796.522'3—dc23

                                        2011029207

♻ Printed on recycled paper

ISBN (paperback): 978-1-59485-500-9
ISBN (ebook): 978-1-59485-501-6

Contents

Acknowledgments

A book such as this requires the help of many, many other people. I would like to begin by thanking the staff at The Mountaineers Books for proposing the project and helping me see it through to completion, especially the work of Kate Rogers and Mary Metz. A special thanks goes to the photographers who contributed their work, capturing the magic of the sport of bouldering through their lenses. Without the efforts of Andy Mann, Andrew Burr, Andrew Kornylak, Caroline Treadway, Jackie Hueftle, Shannon Forsman, and Tim Kemple, this would have been a much poorer book. Also I want to thank the writers who contributed their thoughts on the sport of bouldering. Master boulderers John Gill, Dave Graham, Fred Nicole, Marc Le Menestrel, Ben Moon, Daniel Woods, Ty Landman, Alex Johnson, and Jamie Emerson all gave generously of their time and energy. Thanks to Kurt Smith, Michael Kennedy, and John Gill

for their photographs. Conversations with Christian Griffith, Lynn Hill, Joe Kinder, Matt Samet, Abbey Smith, Jason Kehl, Jimmy Webb, Alex Johnson, Angie Payne, Chris Schulte, Chris Danielson, Eric Harrison, Dave Wahl, Justen Sjong, Kerwin Klein, Chuck Fryberger, Keith Bradbury, Wills Young, Kevin Jorgeson, and many more helped clarify my thoughts and gave important perspectives on different aspects of the sport. I hope I have done some justice to their contributions to the sport.

This book has arisen in part from many years of bouldering with some of the world's best climbers, many of whom have stayed at some point in Boulder, Colorado. There are so many figures I have learned so much from over this time. Johnny Dawes, Ian Powell, and Pat Ament have always had the gift of seeing outside the mainstream perspective. Rob Candelaria has been so generous with his gym to many climbers, myself included, creating a kind of climbing laboratory that has proved a key to the scene here in Boulder and, by extension, the entire world. Thanks also go to the great people at The Spot, where a number of photos were taken for the book, as well as to the Boulder Rock Club, which has supported me for many years. Thanks to Josh Helke at Organic Climbing, Ben at Moon Climbing, and Five Ten shoes for their excellent products. Michael Kennedy, Katie Ives, and Keese Lane have helped foster my writing career in a way I could not have predicted five years ago. A special thanks also goes to John Sherman, whose writings on the sport of bouldering have provided continuous inspiration.

Finally I would like to thank friends and family who have helped support what is now more than thirty years of climbing. Thanks go especially to my parents, who gave me the freedom to explore rock climbing as a child. Without their support, I would never have experienced the joys of climbing and the memories it has created. Most of all, thanks to my wife Caolan and daughter Sophia for supporting this seemingly endless project with affection and good humor. Without them, this book would never have happened.

Foreword

I started bouldering as soon as I started rock climbing. In the gym, I toproped the first two or three things I did, but soon I was on the bouldering wall trying to practice my footwork. At that point in my life, bouldering was the only way to learn how to rock climb because I had too much energy for another partner. I started off just practicing. I looked at bouldering as a way to go about what I was trying to do by myself, without bothering anybody, just doing it in a comfortable area, where it didn't feel dangerous. Bouldering was my way of interpreting climbing. Since there was so little climbing in Portland, Maine, where I grew up, I learned to climb by bouldering.

Bouldering is essential to climbing. There is no experience in climbing where bouldering cannot play some part. Every single time I am about to tie in to a rope, I might be bouldering around the base of the wall, maybe warming up out of boredom, maybe just out of sheer interest, maybe because there are lots of interesting features.

Bouldering is like that. You're not going from start to finish and clipping the chains. There are boulder problems out there that are traverses, and boulder problems that are two moves. There are miniature boulders, and there are gigantic boulders that are actually free solos. It's very undefined. I started to learn through that process.

I began to learn how to boulder in Pawtuckaway and Lincoln Woods in Rhode Island. In the years that followed I started to climb V10s on rock. I took trips to go bouldering, not rock climbing, in the Gunks. I think we were the first generation of climbers for whom it was cool to boulder. Now it's cool to climb V10 in the gym. But we climbed V6 in the gym; V6 was cool to us. It was about the action; it was about the experience; and it was about the process of learning how to create problems to use in advancing yourself as a climber. It was about using rock to learn how to climb it. We became better climbers because we bouldered.

Bouldering can be interpreted differently for each person. It's like art, like music. You can push it in many different directions. You look at a whole new section of rock, all kinds of different rock. You don't look at cliffs, or at El Cap, Mount Everest, or Annapurna. You look at the base of everything, you look all over everything. You look into the middle of Mount Everest or Annapurna. You look in the middle of the cliff, you look in the middle of El Cap. Bouldering means you look at something other than routes.

Bouldering is a way to prove to myself that I can understand different types of rock. It gives me experience that I can apply to anything I want to climb. When I moved to Switzerland, I said "I will put up a bunch of really hard boulder problems." I saw the potential and I knew how to put them up. I knew how to clean them, make them climbable. I had learned. There are many things you have to be careful about. You have to know how to open boulder problems.

Really special bouldering areas are those that offer more than just climbing. The geology, the setting, the movement, and much more make these places important. Too many climbers seem to visit special places just to fill in their 8a scorecards. Look at Chaos Canyon and consider how many times the boulders have moved. Though we are climbing there now, it's so ephemeral. This is a canyon of rock

with glaciers in it. Everything moves. A *problem* I put up in Sustenpass in Switzerland was buried in an avalanche. Everything changes, even El Cap. Go to Rocky Mountain National Park and realize that it has become a brand new area to certain climbers over time, even though many others have climbed there for many years. It was reinvented, renewed. Every person who goes up there with a new attitude can discover new problems. It's all about your vision. Whatever you think is possible. Places are special when you can perceive what is special about them.

It was awe-inspiring to visit Chaos Canyon for the first time. I had never seen a landscape like that. It was the first time I had been in the mountains. We were staring at it every day. It was pristine beauty and we were just happy to be up there. We were terrified of the lightning storms. It was really scary, adventurous, and radical. It's amazing that people can go up there and not see how super cool it is, instead focusing on the grades and the numbers.

Particular boulders stand out. Special problems seem to come in little collectives. On one boulder you can find *Dreamtime* and *The Story of Two Worlds*. The scoop right next to it and the back wall has a V16 *project* on it. There's one phenomenal block with projects still to do. Good pieces of rock lend themselves to really good problems, though sometimes they may only have one problem. Collectives of perfect rock. *Suspension of Disbelief, Polish Terrorist, La Beleine,* so many good problems, of all grades, all over the world. All I've done in my climbing career is look for good problems.

I have to concentrate when finding positions and moving properly because I'm not the most powerful person. Climbing harder is not about choosing between mental and physical approaches. Bouldering is a complete synchronization of physical and mental existence. With this attitude, I can journey wherever I want. For me, bouldering at the highest levels hinges on figuring out how to move. I don't know other ways to do it. I can only try so many times until I realize that I need to, say, move my hips to the left. I see other climbers try and then say they are going to the gym to train for a week. But will they climb better when things get complicated?

Learning to climb better, that's why I boulder. Realizations in rock climbing can range from minute to massive. The process of learning to climb is the engine, the fundamental drive behind a lot of it. You pull on the wall to realize what you want to do. Maybe you realize you are not trying hard enough. Do you need to learn how to toehook better? Should you heelhook instead of toehook? Should you just climb it frontally? Or have you missed something else altogether? Bouldering is within your power. Create your own reality.

I grew up spending a lot of time on the beach. I liked to look for stuff, rocks. I have done this my whole life, only now I'm looking for bigger rocks, cliffs, boulders. I'm into cool exquisite pieces of rock. I don't know how they were formed but they are perfect. What nature does is impossible for us to recreate. Appreciating what is out there is vital.

You've got a dream; make it happen. There are V15s everywhere, and they start by mixing nature and your imagination.

— *Dave Graham*

John Gill bouldering at Dixon Springs circa 1964. (Photo courtesy Gill Collection)

The Gifts of Bouldering: A Commentary by John Gill

Modern bouldering as we know it would not exist without the pioneering spirit of John Gill. By applying the mindset and training techniques of gymnastics to climbing, he was the first in the United States to focus entirely on bouldering as a pursuit in its own right. A humble and insightful observer of the sport, his modesty completely belies the contributions he has made to the world of climbing.

What was bouldering like in America more than half a century ago? To begin with, there were, at most, a few thousand serious rock climbers, some of whom practiced their climbing skills on small rocks, sometimes with top ropes, sometimes without. In the eastern United States and Midwest, most boulder, or outcrop climbing, was geared to mountaineering although there were some attempts at pushing difficulty levels. It was not unusual to see climbers on a 20-foot section of rock burdened with heavy packs and wearing mountain boots. In the far West a more competitive atmosphere encouraged tackling levels of difficulty one might find on new and longer rock climbs, rather than alpine excursions.

The distinction between toproping and bouldering was vague and casual then, and the common descriptor was practice climbing. There were no bouldering pads— the technology of the time produced only extremely heavy and cumbersome gymnastics mats. Nor was there a compelling interest in risk while at play on local rocks. Highballing was a concept that became popular years later. Although some climbers point to my 1961 ascent of *The Thimble* as setting the stage, I never considered *The Thimble* a boulder problem but instead an effort to test my limits as a soloist. In my mind, there was a clear distinction between soloing—what we now call free soloing— and bouldering.

The prevailing attitude was that bouldering, or practice climbing, was a divertissement where serious attempts at excellence were entertained but in a playful sense and entirely separate from "real" climbing. A defeat on a Yosemite wall might provoke hostility and depression, but failure on a boulder problem resulted merely in gentle ribbing and was soon forgotten. As a sport, bouldering was a wraith, devoid of consequence—and hence substance—but nevertheless an amusing activity on an off-day.

For the few of us who took bouldering a bit more seriously, the world was fresh and new, with exciting opportunities for exploration—the heart of the sport at the time—not only at traditional climbing areas, but in the flatlands where little bits of rock appeared and where no one had ever thought of climbing. There were so many potential bouldering gardens, so many formations awaiting the application of one's imagination, that we rarely spent more than an hour or so on any single project. A decade and a half later, in the mid-1970s, the next generation of boulderers, with Colorado's Jim Holloway in the vanguard, would refine our sport and begin spending hours, days, even weeks working on a particular problem—even a single move on a boulder—to advance difficulty levels.

My unique perspective of bouldering and rock climbing as an extension of formal gymnastics emphasized fluid and graceful performance—kinesthetics—as well as pure difficulty. Furthermore, throughout my career as a climber I practiced bouldering as a form of moving meditation. Nevertheless, even though Holloway, Pat Ament, and a few others accepted the notion of process as an integral part of bouldering accomplishment, later generations reverted to the singular quest of difficulty.

What does bouldering offer now, not merely to the elites at the far end of the athletic spectrum, but to normal climbers? An engagement with the rock at any level of difficulty demands a synthesis of the physical and the mental that far transcends normal experience, hones the ability to think clearly under extraordinary physical strain, and requires focusing attention completely on the task at hand. A boulderer enters a private but intense zone no matter how many companions are present. And it is great exercise to boot!

Popular bouldering gardens provide scales of difficulty that climbers can use to assess progress. Yet exploration of new terrain can be as exciting as it was a century ago. And what boulderer has not experienced that subtle and delightful shift of reality when returning to a vexing problem and finding the unaltered rock more accommodating?

Mystical? Hardly...but an exciting journey along a vertical path.

— *John Gill*

Introduction: The Essence of Climbing

In the late 1950s, a young John Gill had been roaming across the open expanses of the Rocky Mountain West, finding adventure less among the snowy peaks and grand ridges that his peers sought out than among the boulder fields and small cliffs below the big walls. One of his favorite places was the Black Hills of South Dakota, a fairyland of pinnacles, crags, and walls composed of richly featured crystalline rock. Among this forest of stone, he found *The Thimble*, a 30-foot formation right next to a popular climbers' parking lot. Something about this formation caught his eye: a potential route up its gently overhung north face.

He began to explore the wall, climbing up and coming back down. There was no protection to speak of. A wooden guardrail ensured a disastrous landing if he fell. He could have toproped the line, but something stopped him from taking this step. Little by little, making long drives from the air force station where he was based in Montana, and

training with one-arm pull-ups in the gym whenever he could, he finally committed to the irreversible upper half of the route, *onsight* and alone. In 1961, without a rope, he created what may well have been the hardest free climb in the world. It was a monument to skill and vision that went unrepeated for almost thirty years.

In the heart of Yosemite Valley, in the middle of Camp 4, the famous climbers' campground, rests a granite behemoth called the Columbia Boulder. An established bouldering circuit had already emerged on the Valley floor in the mid-1950s, but on the black-streaked overhanging north wall a new frontier waited. A series of unobvious features, including the infamous lightning-bolt hold, led to an unlikely lip encounter and the upper slab. Jon Yablonski pointed out the line to two Valley free-climbing stars, John Bachar and Ron Kauk, who began to *work* the moves. In 1978, after numerous hard falls, Kauk turned the lip on the infamous top mantel and *Midnight Lightning*, perhaps still the most famous boulder problem in the world, was born. Its V8 rating (nowadays considered only about midpoint in the popular boulder difficulty rating system) belies the seriousness of

Kurt Smith on the fourth ascent of Midnight Lightning, *Yosemite* (Kurt Smith Collection)

the problem as its height, complexity, and committing nature keep aspirants at bay, even in the era of large pads and sticky rubber.

In the mid-1990s sport climbing had taken hold of the international climbing scene. Long endurance routes and competitions were the vogue. But Frédéric Nicole had taken another path, seeking the hardest moves he could do on rock. On an isolated and obscure boulder deep in the Swiss Alps, near the village of Branson, Nicole had been working on a short but fierce series of moves out a blank overhanging wall. With the physique of a wrestler, unparalleled finger crimping strength, and a quiet and unassuming demeanor, Nicole opened the gates to the realm of modern high-level bouldering with ascents at the V13 and V14 levels. *Radja*, the first V14 in the world, remains a significant accomplishment for serious boulderers even today. For the next decade, Nicole traveled around the world, and today, the United States, South Africa, and Australia are among the places transformed by this climber's vision of the possible.

These are just a few of the many stories from the history of bouldering, a sport that has transformed the face of climbing across its many subdisciplines. Bouldering has always been about discovering the overlooked, solving the impossible, and breaking barriers and limits. Reducing the act of climbing to its most essential aspects, stripping away the distractions, and discovering hidden potential of the rock itself; these are the principles at the heart of bouldering.

Adie Drolet at Carter Lake, Colorado (Photo by Andy Mann)

WHAT IS BOULDERING?

Bouldering is a form of climbing that focuses on climbing relatively short routes, typically unroped and often, but not necessarily, with the pursuit of difficulty as its primary goal. It can be practiced anywhere climbable features exist, such as at the bottom of a cliff, on a small outcropping of rock, or even on a short constructed climbing wall or building. At the heart of bouldering is the search for solutions to difficult sections of rock, hence the frequent use of the word *problem* rather than *route* when describing these climbable sections.

In mainstream rock climbing, the challenges are often routefinding, sequence solving, protecting the leader, and other technical issues. In bouldering, routefinding and sequencing are rarely issues. All climbers are leaders and all falls are relatively short groundfalls. The problem may consist merely of trying to hang onto one hold and making a single move to another. Boulderers delight in seeking out the smallest refinements that transform the impossible into the merely difficult, upping the ante every time in terms of application of strength and intelligence to meet the challenge of maybe only one or two additional moves forward.

Focused on the rock and not the protection, the climber who boulders becomes ever more aware of the nuances of different rock types and the sensations of fingers and feet, and more in tune with the ambient environment: the sun, humidity, and wind moving past the wall. By attempting single moves or short sequences, climbers can learn specialized moves and build strength at an accelerated rate, applying those skills to longer climbs as desired.

Bouldering is also about freedom. Freed of ropes, most gear, and major objective dangers, you can choose to climb alone or with a group of climbers, to stick to one boulder or climb several in an afternoon. The freedom to define your own goals in climbing and to achieve them without excessive investment in equipment is another great attraction, especially when compared to the strictures of big-wall climbing or mountaineering.

The primary allure of bouldering for many is its simplicity. Once everything is stripped away, you are left with what Ben Moon, the famous British climber and boulderer, calls "the essence of climbing." You are alone with a piece of stone molded by time and the elements, to make of it what you will, with no need to answer to anyone else about what you climb, how you climb, or when you climb. As ace boulderer Jimmy Webb says, "I tend to obtain happiness in simple acts such as completing a move I viewed as difficult, or just plain being out in the woods. It's amazing to me how just being out with that right group of friends sends your psych meter through the roof." Most climbers who choose to boulder would agree.

WHY BOULDER?

At its inception, bouldering was commonly considered practice climbing, something you did on rainy days or as a diversion.

John Gill changed this perception radically, building a vision of bouldering as an end in itself, with no need to justify its existence in the context of a larger goal.

When I started climbing and bouldering, I had trouble finding climbers whose vision of bouldering coincided with my own. Today bouldering is entirely an end in itself, with professional climbers who do nothing but boulder. Boulderers travel for months on end visiting boulder fields around the world, from the United States to Switzerland to South Africa.

Bouldering on constructed walls has its own dedicated following, attracting climbers who are connoisseurs of certain particular products, holds for walls, or individual route setters. These climbers find as much fulfillment in indoor sessions at the local gym or on their own home wall as others might find in outdoor climbing on natural rock at a bouldering mecca like Hueco Tanks.

The purity of beautiful movement that a good boulder problem offers inspires climbers to dedicate their time, energy, and money to bouldering. Regardless of how hard a problem is, the best boulder problems offer movement on beautiful features and movement distilled to its essential nature. It is a climbing medium that justifies obsession as the boulderer ceaselessly refines his skills and strategies to resolve a difficult move or sequence. Colorado climber Chris Schulte describes bouldering this way: "It's meditative and physical, revealing many layers and deeper levels of understanding. Bouldering engages problem solving and creativity, and gets one outside." Whether on a beat-up urban boulder or a pristine chunk of alpine granite, the attraction is the same: one of divining the relationship between body and rock in the vertical and overhanging world.

For many boulderers, the social element is vital to the sport. A boulder problem can be tried by a group of climbers who collaborate and support each other in the process of solving the problem, building social cohesion and camaraderie. With the element of risk from falling kept to a minimum, spirits seem higher, more buoyant, and relaxed, raising climbers' aspirations and abilities.

WHY READ THIS BOOK?

Nothing seems simpler than finding a rock somewhere and climbing it. Yet bouldering has generated some of the most interesting writing in the literature of climbing. It is a pursuit that lends itself to reflection, analysis, and expression.

This book explores bouldering as part of a process of learning about climbing, to help you to become a better climber and to consider thoughtfully the ways in which you climb.

Bouldering: Movement, Tactics, and Problem Solving also attempts to answer some of the hard questions that lie in wait for all serious climbers. What is the right balance between security and danger? Can I trust this hold? How do I best resolve this boulder problem? These are questions answered by looking within, and by relying on instinct, understanding, and awareness. I hope that this book can help steer you to this state of self-reliance and self-awareness for a long, happy career in climbing.

A NOTE ABOUT SAFETY

Safety is an important concern in all outdoor activities. No book can alert you to every hazard or anticipate the limitations of every reader. The descriptions of techniques and procedures in this book are intended to provide general information. This is not a complete text on bouldering technique. Nothing substitutes for formal instruction, routine practice, and plenty of experience. When you follow any of the procedures described here, you assume responsibility for your own safety. Use this book as a general guide to further information. Under normal conditions, excursions into the backcountry require attention to traffic, road and trail conditions, weather, terrain, the capabilities of your party, and other factors. Keeping informed about current conditions and exercising common sense are the keys to a safe, enjoyable outing.

— *The Mountaineers Books*

CHAPTER 1

Welcome to Bouldering

People have likely clambered on rocks since the beginning. Yet rock climbing as a sport did not begin to seriously develop until the middle of the nineteenth century. The concept of bouldering was an outgrowth of this new interest in rock. English and European climbing books of the time make passing references to climbing on small outcrops and boulders, usually in the context of practicing for bigger cliffs and routes.

THE EARLY HISTORY OF BOULDERING

Modern bouldering probably originated not far from the city of Paris, France, on the sandstone rocks in the forests of Fontainebleau, where thousands of excellent sandstone boulders lie under extensive pine forests, creating a convenient and beautiful place to climb. By the end of the 1920s, Fontainebleau was an established climbing area with a dedicated cadre of climbers who established individual boulder problems as well as link-ups of boulder problems called *circuits*. Though for most climbers such climbing was still "practice" for alpine peaks or bigger walls, a number began to specialize in bouldering for its own sake. These climbers became known as *bleausards*, and the best known of them, Pierre Allain, would invent the first specialized rock climbing footwear, which was named after his initials, the P.A. It would not be the last time that important innovation came from the practice of bouldering.

Bouldering was also practiced early on in the British Isles, where numerous low outcroppings and boulders made a logical place for the sport, especially in the Peak District in England on its signature gritstone. While there is no question that during this time European climbers were operating at the highest levels of free-climbing difficulty, it was in Great Britain that the idea of pure rock climbing, with no summit or mountaineering objective as a goal and no "aid," or artificial means of ascent, began to truly take hold.

Bouldering as we know it today began to emerge in the 1960s in the United States through the efforts of one individual, John Gill. John Gill was crucial to the development of the sport. He came to the sport from gymnastics so he thought about the act of climbing in terms of physical form and levels of difficulty. In gymnastics, the apparatus stays constant, meaning innovation and invention comes from the performer. There is also a generally recognized scale of difficulty for certain positions and movements. Gill was the first to recognize

that climbing could be approached in a similar way. A climber could seek out very specific movements or sequences of holds, disregarding the idea of a route with a summit destination in favor of that of a problem, how to sequence through a series of upward moves. Gill's background as a professor of mathematics meant he brought close mental analysis to his bouldering. Problems could be rated on a scale Gill called the B-grade rating system.

Gill looked at the pursuit outside the typical perspectives of the day, which were fixed on bigger objectives such as big-wall climbing or mountaineering. He developed the idea of bouldering as a type of climbing that consciously avoided risk. In doing so he raised the difficulty level of climbing—people were able to climb much harder routes when not risking serious injury—in the United States to V8 or V9 at a time when the hardest routes of the day were perhaps mid-5.10 to easy 5.11, which roughly equaled perhaps V1 or V2 at the cruxes. This was a phenomenal achievement, a leap forward of unprecedented proportions. The climbing world saw the future in his ascent of *The Thimble*, a ground-up solo of a mid-5.12 route in 1961. Done without bolts, *The Thimble* showed that a climber with dedicated training and a high-level of gymnastic ability could ascend routes on overhanging face climbing of much higher difficulty. Yet it would

John Gill bouldering at Shades Mountain in Alabama in the 1960s. (Photo courtesy Gill Collection)

be almost thirty years before the new era of sport climbing began. Gill set the path toward hard sport climbing as well as bouldering; he just didn't use bolts.

Gill's contributions certainly didn't end there, however. He introduced chalk for keeping a climber's hand dry for gripping holds. Gill also developed the type of dynamic yet controlled movement that would utterly transform the sport. Both innovations put the focus squarely on the climber, not the gear, radically changing not just the practice but the appearance of the sport forever.

The last and perhaps most important innovation wrought by Gill was the idea of actual physical training for rock climbing. Gill came into gymnastics after some experience climbing and saw the potential for applying gymnastics training in developing climbing strength. For most climbers, such an approach was unpopular and was even seen as unethical until well into the 1980s. Yet pictures of Gill doing one-arm front levers and one-finger pull-ups, published in Pat Ament's legendary 1977 biography of Gill, *Master of Rock*, inspired many others to try to do the same. Much of today's emphasis on physical strength and strength training can be traced to Gill's influence.

Ultimately, Gill's greatest legacy was his approach to climbing. Understated, honest, and serious, Gill sought out new problems that brought out a climber's best. Many are now area classics that dedicated boulderers travel long distances to try. Gill also wrote thoughtful and eloquent prose about what he believed his style of climbing had to

offer. Any serious climber can learn a great deal from reading Gill's writings on bouldering, including "The Art of Bouldering," published in 1969 in the American Alpine Club Journal.

BOULDERING AFTER 1970: THE MODERN ERA

By 1970, John Gill had laid the foundations and bouldering began to be taken more seriously, with centers of activity emerging, especially in Colorado and California. Pat Ament was a very important presence in Colorado in the 1960s and early 1970s, establishing a number of classic hard problems and exposing climbers to the sport through his writing.

Among the most remarkable individuals of this era was a tall, incredibly strong individual named Jim Holloway who, in a number of forays in the hills west of Boulder, established problems that may well have been V12 or V13, very tough grades at the time, which went unmatched in the United States until the mid-1990s. *Trice* on Flagstaff Mountain remains a respected test piece, not repeated for some thirty years after its first ascent. *Meathook* and *Slapshot* remain unrepeated, though the latter, sadly, is broken.

In California two major names emerged, John Bachar and Ron Kauk, as well as the premier chronicler of American rock climbing, John Long. Kauk's ascent of *Midnight Lightning* in Yosemite Valley was a breakthrough, not so much for difficulty as for its striking aesthetics. For years afterward, an

Jim Holloway on Trice *at Flagstaff Boulder, Colorado in the 1970s* (Photo by Rob Candelaria)

ascent of *Midnight Lightning* was a mandatory entrance exam for serious bouldering, and even today it carries a reputation for difficulty and seriousness that far outweighs its V8 grade.

In the 1980s a few new things emerged to change the sport once more, pushing the technical standards higher. Gyms and artificial walls, sticky climbing shoe rubber, landing or crashpads, and the V-grade rating system enabled climbers to push limits, techniques, and terrain to

unheard-of heights. Of these perhaps the artificial wall was most significant. Climbers were suddenly able to design challenges and set routes in a few minutes that might take years to find outside, and these inside boulder problems were accessible regardless of weather or time of day. The ability to practice strength, technique, and endurance in a controlled environment radically democratized the sport. Climbers could emerge from inside climbing gyms located in flat states such as Florida or Ohio and prove themselves in traditional, open-air testing grounds in Colorado or California.

Crashpads carried the environment of the gym to the outdoors, allowing safe passage in previously hazardous terrain. Using four or five pads allowed much safer falls and absolute focus on the difficulty of the problem. Low overhangs in alpine talus, previously regarded as unclimbable or insignificant, emerged as the proving ground for a new generation. A new moniker emerged to describe boulderers: pad people.

Bouldering grades also were vital to transforming bouldering. In the 1960s and 1970s, bouldering difficulty was described in a number of ways, most famously the B-grade rating system of John Gill. B3 was the top grade, representing a problem unrepeated, despite the efforts of the recognized strong climbers of the day. This scheme, however, was too imprecise to give a true description of a problem's challenges. It was not until the late 1980s and early 1990s, after bouldering began to take off in Hueco Tanks in Texas, that climber John Sherman, in his first guidebook to the area,

John Long, Largo Pinch Overhang, *Horsetooth Reservoir, Colorado* (Photo by Michael Kennedy)

introduced an absolute scale of difficulty, a number from 1 to 16 linked with a V, from Sherman's nickname, "Vermin."

The V-scale was the more consistent and comparable ratings system that was needed to more precisely assess boulder problems. Not surprisingly, hours are spent debating the ratings of problems, reflecting how factors such as variations in a climber's height or reach, or *conditions* on-site can radically affect perceptions of difficulty.

By the mid-1990s, the bouldering landscape began to change radically as new talent at home and abroad—climbers such as Chris Sharma, Dave Graham, and Frédéric Nicole—rapidly established problems at the V13 grade and higher. In Europe and the United States, new areas such as Ticino in Switzerland and the boulders around Bishop, California, were discovered and old ones such as Fontainebleau and Hueco redeveloped. Bouldering competitions became more popular than roped sport climbing competitions in the United States, and it was possible to become a sponsored athlete in what had previously been seen as a small niche carved out of the bigger sport of climbing. New companies catered to this new crowd, producing crashpads, climbing holds, and most strikingly, clothing and accessories that emulated the urban trends of skateboard and hip-hop cultures.

By the mid-2000s, climbing had begun to cross over to become a mainstream sport, a process fostered by the accessibility of bouldering. With the arrival of inexpensive HD video cameras and YouTube, a beginning boulderer could choose from thousands of

Daniel Woods in action at Rocky Mountain National Park (Photo by Caroline Treadway)

videos of problems all over the world, an educational tool of unprecedented power. Kids were increasingly organized into youth teams, regional and national competition series were organized, and in some locales, indoor bouldering became like soccer or any other typical school sport. Media exposure of new problems became instantaneous, as climber blogs, news sites, and social media broadcast the latest hard *sends* and successful ascents the day they were done and live feeds of bigger competitions became standard.

This explosive growth has not been without problems, especially in the natural environments where bouldering has always found its deepest inspiration. Hueco Tanks, once the reserve of a dedicated few, is now heavily crowded in prime season, with a reservation system and climber escorts required in parts of the park. The impact of climber visits on high alpine areas is debated in Colorado, and access issues continue to plague significant areas in the Northeast. Other issues remain in the background, especially the debate as to whether the commercialization and competitive aspects of the new face of climbing

Andy Salo on the first ascent of Edge of Oblivion *(V7), Rocky Mountain National Park*
(Photo by Andy Mann)

are ultimately destructive, undermining the intrinsic values of an activity that brings together mind, body, and nature in moments of rich and intense beauty. What the future holds for access and management is unclear. Yet the fundamental appeal of the sport—movement on rock and engaging with the infinitely variable forms of the natural world—will always remain at its heart.

ENVIRONMENT AND ETHICS

Part of the game of bouldering is respecting your fellow climber and the natural world and acting ethically toward both. The growing popularity of the sport of bouldering puts an increasing burden on outdoor bouldering areas. Your ethics and climbing style affect not only the bouldering environment but the experience of other people (climbers, visitors, and landowners). Learning to minimize environmental impacts and treat others with respect is part of learning how to boulder well.

The most important goal any boulderer can aim for is to leave as little trace of her passage as possible. Leave No Trace (LNT) should be the foundational ethical principle of every climber. Every action should be considered carefully for its individual as well as cumulative impact. If each person removes one plant, or a part of a plant, soon little remains.

Biking, carpooling, or public transportation reduces the environmental impact of getting to your destination. On the *approach*, climbers should follow established trails, not cut switchbacks, and minimize erosion by sticking to hardened surfaces such as talus or snow instead of vegetated areas. At the boulders, following LNT practices means leaving your gear in places that don't have vegetation and keeping it close together rather than spread out. Careful use of pads can limit the destruction of vegetation at the boulder's base.

Personal behavior can profoundly affect not only those around you, but the wildlife at the boulders as well. Playing amplified music, shouting, and cursing is not only obnoxious to other climbers and nearby visitors but can stress wildlife and affect their ability to care for young or find food. Smoking is annoying to nonsmokers in the vicinity and carries with it the risk of starting wildfires. Leave dogs at home when visiting any popular area. While climbing, you won't be able to attend to them, and,

left to their own, some dogs will chase wildlife, harass other boulderers, make noise, and cause pollution and erosion by defecating around the boulder field and trampling plants off-trail. Don't leave trash, tape, or other human-caused debris at the boulders.

To help the cause of bouldering and maintain access to privately owned areas or in public areas, it's important to behave as responsible visitors. Courteous driving through town with a friendly wave to locals and patronizing of local shops and restaurants; careful parking; discreet approaches to the boulders: All will be noticed and appreciated. Illegal camping, trespassing, shouting, fires, and so on will also be noticed, and will send the message that bouldering cannot be tolerated. The choice is simple and yours to make. Visit the Access Fund's website at www.accessfund .org to find out more on how you can be a good steward of the boulders.

In a world increasingly crowded with artificial experiences, part of the challenge in bouldering outside is to accept the limitations imposed by the natural world and make them an integral part of the game. Climbing should always be done with the goal of preserving the natural features of the boulders. Never alter the shape of the holds to make a move easier. If loose rock needs to be removed, it should be done with a minimum of force and as cleanly as possible. Leave lichens and moss alone. No boulder problem should involve stripping of vegetation. Find another problem, if necessary; there are often many to choose from. It is better to confine *cleaning* of a problem to the specific holds required. Remember to use only nylon bristle brushes for cleaning holds. Trees should be preserved and worked around with any trimming of branches thought through carefully. Vegetation stabilizes surface soil and if removed may result in increasingly worse landings through erosion.

It has become popular to modify landings beneath boulders, removing rocks or making the ground flatter. In some instances, this kind of modification is acceptable, particularly in stabilizing popular but eroded areas. In any event, such alteration should only be done with the full approval of the climbing community and land management agencies or owners. Independent alteration of climbing environments, such as creating new trails or modifying landings, can quickly create serious access problems.

Once the *session* is over, remove gear of any kind, including pads. Although for many this practice is seen as merely a matter of personal preference rather than a genuine environmental issue, stashed pads often wind up deteriorating in the weather and being chewed by marmots or other animals, creating a mess and a wildlife hazard. The passage of time and the decisions of land managers will ultimately settle the debate.

BOULDERING STYLE

Rules concerning style deal with climbing a problem once the other issues of environment and ethics have been resolved. What defines "correct" style prompts numerous debates, and consensus has not been reached on many topics. To an outsider, it might seem like debating the number of angels that can fit on the head of a pin; but to boulderers it is no different than quarrels in other areas of climbing, be it the use of supplemental oxygen to climb Everest or placing new bolts on El Capitan.

Style can be divided itself into two main areas, working the problem and actually doing the problem. Let's look at issues associated with working the problem. Among the most contentious is cleaning holds and working out moves on a tall boulder problem while on *toprope*. This tactic, called *headpointing*, was developed in Great Britain on cliffs where bolts and other fixed gear are not permitted. Some argue that headpointing reduces adventure and takes opportunity away from climbers who want to go ground up on first ascents. Outside of first ascents, this issue seems up to the discretion of the individual, and as long as this tactic is disclosed, other climbers won't care too much. If it was good enough for John Gill, who worked in both modes, it's good enough for anybody else.

Starting holds and how one begins a boulder problem is another topic of style. Many problems have had lower starts added to them over time, and in a number of places, such as Hueco Tanks, those new versions have earned their own name and grade. In other situations, problems have been customarily started with blocks of stone, or *cheatstones* (now usually replaced by stacked pads), used to reach the first holds of a problem. The solution is disclosure as to which *start* was used. Some problems are agonizingly specific with regard to starting position and holds; the best bet is to learn the rules for any given problem. Issues only arise when climbers are perceived as claiming ascents that don't conform to the accepted style for a problem.

Working tactics such as using stacked pads to inspect or try individual moves higher on a problem or getting a *power spot*, (hands-up help) are seen these days more as normal practices rather than stylistic transgressions. Most common nowadays is doing whatever is necessary to work moves or climb safely as long as it doesn't harm the environment or affect other climbers.

Despite this anything-goes attitude, a straightforward, unassisted first-try ascent of a hard problem is both highly regarded by others and hugely satisfying to the climber. Borrowing terms from sport climbing, bouldering has adopted the ideas of *onsighting* or *flashing* problems. Onsighting is an ascent of a problem on your first try, ground up, with no prior knowledge of sequences or holds. The second, the flash, is simply a first-try ascent with previous knowledge. An on-sight ascent of a hard boulder problem commands the highest respect, especially if the problem is committing or tall. The pursuit of *highballs* is a recognized subset of the sport of bouldering, though one that carries with it considerable risks, since boulderers climb unprotected by rope, pieces, or anchors.

Despite debates, the majority of boulderers accept a fairly common set of rules and ethics, and only ascents done within this framework are recognized as legitimate. *Chipping* holds, falsifying ascents, destroying vegetation, disrupting wildlife, and generally ignoring fellow climbers and the environment are harmful to both the natural world and the climbing world. Climb respectfully and the experience will pay rewards far richer than a check on your ticklist.

CHAPTER 2

Gear

One of the most attractive aspects of bouldering is its simplicity and freedom from expensive equipment purchases. Bouldering might not require much gear, but safe and fun bouldering calls for appropriate gear, from clothing and shoes to safety-related equipment such as crashpads. I will also go into the use of each, emphasizing low-impact techniques for bouldering. And although bouldering is already a relatively inexpensive sport, I will show you how to get the best value for your purchase and how to make your gear last longer.

My typical setup, with shoes, different chalk bags, brushes, and a bouldering pad

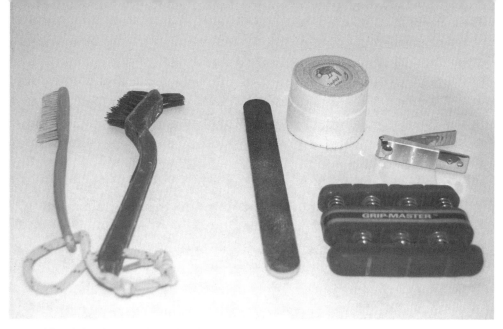

Natural bristle brush, nylon bristle brush, emery board, tape, clippers, and finger exerciser

WHAT YOU NEED AND HOW TO USE IT

From the standpoint of gear, bouldering is the simplest of all climbing disciplines. At its most basic, besides clothing (depending on where you are bouldering, I suppose!), all you need to boulder are a pair of climbing shoes, chalk, and chalkbag. With these you can climb anything from the most modest to the toughest boulder problem.

A typical gear list for a serious boulderer, however, runs as follows:

1. Several pairs of shoes, including comfortable warm-up shoes, lace-up shoes for edging on small holds, and flexible slippers.
2. Chalk and two chalkbags, including a stable chalkpot-style bag to leave on the ground and a portable small one for longer problems such as traverses.
3. Two brushes, including a stiff nylon brush and a natural-bristle brush, to remove chalk and other debris from holds.
4. One or two high-quality bouldering pads, and a carpet square or towel to clean shoes of sand and debris before climbing.
5. Skin-care kit, including nail clippers, athletic tape, antibiotic cream, and an emery board.
6. Clothing such as bouldering-specific pants, shirts, approach shoes, and outerwear.
7. A small pack or bag for carrying miscellaneous items.

This gear list is by no means exhaustive, but it includes most of the things that you need in most bouldering areas.

THE TEN ESSENTIALS:

You won't need most of these when you're bouldering a short distance from your car or the nearest coffee bar but for trips further afield, you may be glad you brought all ten essentials.

1. Navigation (map and compass)
2. Sun protection (sunglasses and sunscreen)
3. Insulation (extra clothing)
4. Illumination (headlamp or flashlight)
5. First-aid supplies
6. Fire (firestarter and matches/lighter)
7. Repair kit and tools (including knife)
8. Nutrition (extra food)
9. Hydration (extra water)
10. Emergency shelter

SHOES

Probably no piece of gear so directly affects climbing success as your shoes, so take your time thinking about your purchase. Learning how they are built and are intended to work is just as much a part of learning to climb as mastering any other piece of gear.

Climbing shoes come in two basic kinds, slip-lasted and board-lasted. The former are the first choice of many boulderers: Slip-lasted shoes are flexible and sensitive, allowing more contact with the holds, however small and irregular. Board-lasted shoes are stiffer, supporting the feet on small edges better but sacrificing feel and sensitivity. They are used primarily for longer routes where protection of the foot and a comfortable fit are a must.

The vast majority of shoes used in bouldering are slip-lasted, low-cut slippers, meaning there is no material covering the ankles and no laces. For slippers to work well they must fit tight as a glove, a process that can only be worked out with the help of a professional, an experienced friend, or trial and error. My way of fitting shoes has always been to size them so I can just barely get them on my feet, and then break them in over two or three weeks wearing the shoes around the house. If you are new to climbing, don't size down too radically at first. Try to get a feel for how the shoes work for you and go from there.

My recommendation for a first bouldering shoe is a slipper with as neutral a fit as possible, a moderate asymmetrical last, and minimal downturn in the toe. An asymmetrical last means that the shoe closely resembles the actual shape of your foot and tends to point to the inside. More advanced shoes often feature a talonlike profile and radically asymmetrical lasts. You will not be able to take advantage of these shoes until you are a fairly proficient climber. High-cut shoes offer better ankle support in the event of a fall, but they limit the flexibility of your foot and ankle, which is especially important when heelhooking or on high-angle problems. Your first shoes as you are learning to boulder should balance performance with a comfortable fit.

Some common mistakes when buying shoes include selecting the wrong kind of shoe, buying used shoes, or using hand-me-down shoes. Board-lasted shoes will

Moderate asymmetrical last and a pronounced downturn make this lace-up a good shoe for precision and support. (Photo courtesy Five Ten)

not help improve bouldering technique as they lack the sensitivity required for good footwork. Used shoes and hand-me-downs are often pretty old, meaning they have been broken in to fit another climber's feet. The materials are compromised as part of the breaking-in process. Shoemaking and design is constantly improving, so new shoes can ultimately be a better investment. Sometimes a really good deal on last year's model turns up. If they fit well, go for it. But don't try to save forty dollars on a pair of shoes that you will never use because they don't fit right.

Don't be influenced by claims of rubber superiority when picking shoes; rubbers these days are roughly equal in terms of friction. Follow your intuition about fit. The shoe that fits the best will let you climb your best. Ask other climbers you know for recommendations but think for yourself.

After you buy those shoes, wear them around the house a few days to confirm they will work. Any reputable store or mail-order company will accept returns on shoes as long as they have not been worn outside, so take your time confirming the fit. Brick-and-mortar stores often allow easier returns, more helpful advice, and a wider selection. Online or mail-order is useful if a store doesn't exist near you.

CHALK AND CHALKBAGS

John Gill is credited with being the first to use gymnastics chalk in rock climbing, and today the use of magnesium carbonate is nearly universal in rock climbing and bouldering. Chalk acts by absorbing sweat, drawing it away from the skin, to leave a much rougher surface with better gripping qualities. For decades, climbers have been carrying small bags of the stuff up with them on climbs of all lengths and styles because it works.

Chalk is widely available from all kinds of sporting goods outlets, not just climbing shops. It can be purchased in block form or pre-ground in bags. Some pre-ground chalks include additives designed to increase the drying power of the chalk. Manufacturers are rarely forthcoming about the actual ingredients in their blends, so you don't often know what you are getting. Try different brands to see what works best for you. I find it's often best to start by buying pure chalk in the block form and breaking it down to your preferred texture.

"Chalk-balls" are designed to minimize the dispersal of loose chalk by binding it in fabric. Because they do not effectively coat fingers well, they are not particularly popular with boulderers, though some gyms require their use. Some climbers use liquid chalk, which is usually magnesium carbonate suspended in rubbing alcohol. Colored chalk, designed to lessen the visual impact of chalk on stone, is also marketed, yet these chalks contain additives that can be slippery and rarely match natural stone well. Colored chalk is not recommended.

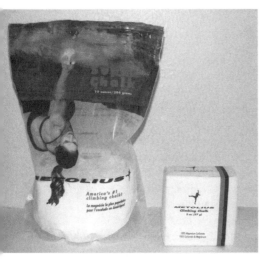

Chalk typically comes pre-crushed in a bag or in block form.

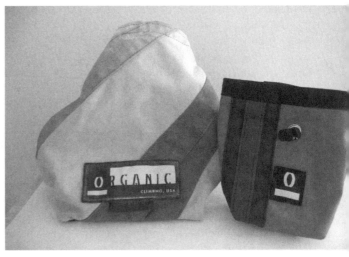

Chalk bucket (or chalkpot) on the left, bag on the right

You may have heard of pof, a resin-based substance used primarily in France and in Fontainebleau in particular. Pof is considered destructive to rock surfaces in most locales as it leaves behind a very thin, slippery, and quasi-permanent layer of resin that cannot be removed by brush or washed away like chalk. Never use pof anywhere in North America. It's best to stick with moderate use of magnesium carbonate and avoid anything else.

Chalkbags are inexpensive and very handy. If you will be bouldering a lot and want only one bag, consider a medium-size bag that will last you on longer boulder problems or even traditional climbing routes. Make sure it can stand upright and remain stable without tipping. Chalkbags will require a belt of some kind; thin accessory cord is easy and secure to tie compared with webbing and buckles. Chalkbags usually come with a sleeve or loop of some kind to carry a toothbrush. Some even come with key pockets.

Consider getting a larger *chalk bucket*— a bag with a handle that is designed to stay upright on the ground—as well. You will also find it handy to have an extra container (plastic storage tubs work well for this) for any chalk not kept in your chalkbag.

After climbing or handling chalk, you will want to clean your hands and moisturize your skin. Inadequate moisturizing can cause finger skin splits, which are surprisingly difficult to heal.

BRUSHES

A dedicated boulderer behaves a bit like a painter in regard to brushes, acquiring many of them over time and dedicating certain ones for certain uses. Three types of brushes are commonly used in bouldering: nylon bristle, natural bristle, and metal bristle. The most common is a simple nylon-bristle toothbrush-style brush (and a simple toothbrush is often used). It's light, versatile and very effective at removing chalk from holds. However, natural, boar-bristle brushes are by far the most effective at cleaning chalk, especially chalk tickmarks, from rock. Every serious boulderer should own at least one. Wire brushes are not used for cleaning chalk from holds so much as cleaning debris including dirt and loose rock from them. The most abrasive, wire brushes are hard on the rock and are usually reserved for first ascents. Wire brushes should never be used on already cleaned holds.

Some climbers will fasten their brush to an extendable aluminum pole, allowing access to out-of-reach holds. In these cases brushes aren't for cleaning chalk: Hard-to-reach holds rarely see much chalk accumulation. However, for less-traveled problems, extended brushes allow removal of dirt, pine needles, broken glass, and other debris that can settle in holds, especially on topouts.

PADS

Nothing has so revolutionized contemporary bouldering as the crashpad. First introduced in America in the mid-1990s, they have become standard equipment for serious boulderers. Crashpads help climbers avoid serious injury. If you keep bouldering,

BOULDERING AT THE HEART OF MY LIFE

Marc Le Menestrel is well known in Europe for his dedication to hard free climbing and bouldering, especially in the forest of Fontainebleau, where he has established problems at the highest levels for years.

I am still so thrilled about going bouldering that I sometimes feel ashamed. After so many years, I could have become more mature, less childish. Alas, I just want to get there, put my shoes on, and start climbing. I feel like our family dog Chouca thirty years ago who was jumping all over the place as soon as we said "Fontainebleau." On the way to the boulders, I flex my fingers like a cowboy preparing for a duel. I connect with nature, searching for the marks left by other climbers on the boulders. I feel the air, in the hope that it will be sufficiently cold so that friction will be good (also, a bit of numbness in the fingers helps you to be less sensitive to pain!). I listen to my body to locate the source of energy that I will be able to use. I am preparing for this vital burst of power that makes me crank a problem or not, a decisive and sometimes brutal catch on the last hold, a way to move that takes root deep inside me, like an animal. To climb a boulder, I like to con- nect with a tiger, a monkey, a snake, or a lizard inside me to find the appropriate power and rhythm the problem requires. It can even be an elephant, because I like to push on my legs as much as I like to pull on my fingers. . . .

There is so much to say: I have experienced bouldering as an alchemy of magical natu- ral places, family ties, tribal friendship, and excessive search for difficulty.

Of course, I am not climbing as difficult boulders as I may once have. But this is not that important, as the thrill of the activity seems to be possible at all level. I also see this with the people around me. They seem addicted regardless of the absolute difficulty of the boulders they climb. In search of difficulty, I like to do boulders beyond my limits. In the past, I have attempted problems without thinking I could ever do them. It is the repetition of many tries in many days that opens doors to the psyche and, sometimes, to hope. A day comes when an undoable boulder becomes possible. Later, it may become a wonderfully surprising achievement. I have surprised myself in bouldering and this has been one of the most beautiful experiences of my life. Bouldering gave me a chance to express myself, to be me beyond myself, in one of the deepest forms and greatest intensities. I feel grateful and wish to live this more. See . . . here I go again, ready for more bouldering!

Marc Le Menestrel

you will find yourself acquiring several of them and using them all.

Pads come in three basic varieties. The first could be called an accessory or half- pad. These are smaller and thinner than full pads. They can provide a spot to clean shoes and start a problem, allowing the use of a full pad elsewhere. They are also used to pad surfaces just outside of the normal fall zone: areas that could risk injury but aren't absolutely necessary to cover. Half-pads should not be expected to provide meaningful protection on tall problems or uneven landings.

The full pad is the workhorse of bouldering. Running about 3 feet by 4 feet and at least 4 inches thick, this is the pad most boulderers use most of the time. They are usually built of heavy-duty nylon, such as Cordura, covering two layers of foam: one thin and relatively stiff, the other thicker and softer. Most full pads come with shoulder carry straps and some form of waist belt.

There are two common varieties of full pads, the taco and the folding-style pad. Taco pads are continuous foam, which makes for a bulkier profile when closed but leaves no thin spots when deployed on the ground. The folding-style pad has a division in the middle allowing easier packing, carrying, and storage but, at the fold, exposes the climber to unpadded landing areas. To eliminate this problem some pads have an angled fold; others feature two pieces of separated thick foam tied together with a continuous layer of thin foam. This hybrid folding pad seems to be more and more standard.

When buying a pad, look for quality workmanship and materials. Are the seams straight and is the stitching securely fastened? Is the exterior material durable? Cheaper pads will use lighter exterior fabric, which will blow apart at the first serious hit or rip on rocks or roots. Pads with carpet or other soft fabric on the landing surface may be less durable in rocky environments. Simple, rugged nylon is durable and acquires less dirt. Bring a small towel to wipe your feet if you want.

Is the interior foam going to handle the load? Cheap pads will have thinner, short-lived foam that will last maybe a season or two at most. Make sure that it is firm: You should be able to step on a pad and feel only a little give. A pad that feels perfectly cushy on the first session will be useless soon. If you are a heavier climber, or if you are bouldering in alpine areas with *talus* landings, for sure you'll want solid, thick foam.

If you are carrying your pad a long way, a good pair of shoulder straps and a decent waist belt will prove invaluable. Think of a pad like a climbing rope. They cost about the same and provide a similar function: a soft, safe catch. Pads are not the place to try to save money on an inferior product.

A final type of bouldering crashpad is the highball. These are thicker and bigger than full pads, allowing safer landings from higher falls. In many situations, two full pads may be more versatile and useful than one highball. But if you are determined to get well off the ground, the extra expense, weight, bulk—and edge of security—of a highball pad may be worth it.

SKINCARE KIT

Boulderers are often amazingly fastidious about skin care. After all, success on a boulder problem, which might be the highlight of a long trip or a season, can hinge on a square millimeter of skin staying in place. Your fingers are vital to climbing well—having the tools to keep finger skin healthy and intact makes sense. A boulderer's skin-care kit includes: nail clippers, an emery board or fine sandpaper, athletic tape, antibiotic ointment, and moisturizer. Store these items in a small bag that closes securely.

Nail clippers are essential for trimming fingernails and removing loose bits of skin sliced by the rock. An emery board or fine sandpaper is used to smooth damaged skin, minimizing the chances of a *flapper*, a piece of fully detached ripped skin that can take days to heal, ruining a trip. Sanding skin helps reduce calluses, improving sensitivity and decreasing the risk of flappers.

A roll of athletic tape has many uses: supporting finger tendons, protecting finger skin on certain sharp holds, bandaging cuts, and even marking holds on problems. Always have tape handy. Some climbers swear by tincture of benzoin to help tape adhere or to toughen skin. Antibiotic ointment keeps torn skin moist and free from infection while hand moisturizer keeps skin pliable and flexible.

CLOTHING

Compared to outfitting for high-altitude mountaineering, the needs for bouldering would seem pretty casual. After all, bouldering doesn't usually involve remote settings or complex approaches and terrain. However, as you become more experienced in the sport, you will notice some things work better than others in bouldering. Let's

look at clothes from top to bottom to see what I mean.

Shirts can be anything that fits and feels right. A simple cotton T-shirt is great in most situations. In situations of cold or damp you may find yourself wishing for a warmer overshirt made of synthetic material. If you are hiking up high in the mountains, a simple fleece pullover might save you from hypothermia when you are rained and hailed on for hours. Just make sure the shirt is relatively loose and nonconfining. Many boulderers don't wear an outer shirt while climbing, even in very cold temperatures, but shirts can help protect you from abrasion.

Likewise with long pants, which can protect you from scrapes and cuts, especially from specialized moves like kneescums and kneebars where shorts would simply be too painful. For maximum freedom of movement, most boulderers prefer loose-fitting cotton pants that breathe well. A gusseted crotch is pretty much standard for climbing wear. Synthetics are popular, but be aware of the slippery aspects of nylon sliding on a crashpad or trying to make a kneebar while slipping on the rock. Cotton has more friction and will stop you quicker, but is a poor insulator, so consider bringing a warm pair of fleece pants if you're heading to the mountains. A well-made pair of climbing pants should serve you well for a number of seasons.

Approach shoes are something to think about, for talus or long hike approaches. Sticky rubber soles are a big plus when scrambling around on rock on the approach, especially when it's wet. Navigating a wet, lichen-covered boulder field in ordinary running shoes while carrying a pad or two can be very dangerous. To wear flip-flops in these situations is completely foolhardy: A seemingly minor thing like a stubbed toe can ruin a day or a trip.

Outerwear includes a waterproof rain jacket, mandatory for alpine areas with frequent summer hail and rain showers, and a puffy down jacket for staying warm between attempts on a problem in mid-winter. A hat is a great idea as well when it's cold out or for keeping the sun off. The main goal is to be able to adapt to the different situations you will encounter, be it roadside in the hot sun or three miles from the trailhead at 11,000 feet.

SMALL BACKPACK OR OTHER CARRY BAG

This is important for carrying the miscellaneous items of your bouldering session: water, food, skincare stuff, food, phone, iPod, and keys.

CHAPTER 3

Paul Robinson tops out on Pinotage *(V10), Rocklands, South Africa.* (Photo by Andy Mann)

Movement in Bouldering

You've been trying the move for an hour now to no avail. Is it finger strength or a foot that just won't stay in place? Something's missing, you think. But on the next try, everything clicks into place, the move goes, and you send the problem. What just happened?

Bouldering is climbing movement, trimmed to its essentials and freed from the constraints of roped climbing: the harness, carabiners, cams, bolts, and other gear needed to protect the climber from long falls. Traditional rock climbing, aid climbing, and ice climbing all filter movement through the protective gear. Free soloing is the exception. Done without extra gear, it has the severest—and, to many, unacceptable—penalty for failure: probable death. While maximum movement efficiency (saving time and covering distances quickly) is imperative on longer routes, it is of little consideration to boulderers. Because of the relative safety of bouldering and the minimal gear, the climber has almost unlimited freedom to explore and experiment with the possibilities of ascent. She can linger, return, and try again as many times as she wants to complete a particular boulder problem.

Bouldering is an exceptionally good way to improve climbing technique, allowing thorough speculation, analysis, and experiment on the best ways to succeed at a move. Falling (safely!) gives instant feedback and speeds the process of sorting out potential solutions to an obstacle.

Minimal preparation is required for attempts. For example, a move may be low enough to allow you to focus on a single hand movement without really leaving the ground. These advantages promote rapid understanding of required positions and movements, keys to moving well on rock.

Lee Payne on Inspect Her Gadget *(V7), Horse Pens 40, Alabama* (Photo by Andy Mann)

FRED NICOLE ON BOULDERING

Fred Nicole is one of the truly transformative figures in the history of climbing, especially bouldering. Nicole is a strong climber and also one of the great explorers of boulder fields, establishing classic new lines in the United States, South Africa, and his native Switzerland. His quiet introspective manner and wisdom make him a real role model to climbers everywhere.

Bouldering is a passion which I have always felt deep within me and which I will never let go of.

I have been climbing for almost thirty years. It is the activity which I have pursued the most consistently in my life. It was also a guiding force which led me through my adolescence and my first steps in adult life. Looking back, I think I found in bouldering a revival of the feelings of childhood: the discovery of new places, of the body and its movements, the wonder and creativity in action, the emotion of surpassing oneself, and, by this, evolving as a climber and an individual human being.

Fred Nicole, the modern master of bouldering, on the Gill Slab at Eldorado Canyon, Colorado (Photo by Andy Mann)

When asked what I remember most about my life in bouldering, it might be the first day in a new area, whether it was twenty years ago at Cresciano or Rocklands or my latest discovery in Switzerland.

In the view of other climbers of the era (when I began), bouldering was training for real climbing. And rock climbing was perceived as a preparation for mountaineering. I began in this fashion and worked on bouldering in order to advance on routes, but I would say that the game of bouldering took priority over my roped climbing. In time what fascinated me most was to open new problems, which has remained the motivation for me today.

Climbing is very diverse so I believe that the most useful path (for improving) is to enlarge one's repertoire of moves with the goal of being able to adapt to the multiple possibilities that the rock offers. After this, depending on your weaknesses and your interests, you can train more specifically for technique, power, flexibility, boldness.... Each day and each problem is different. There are so many different factors. It could be the line, or the social or natural environment. Feelings, people, places, even the light....

For me the simplicity of bouldering remains the aspect which makes it the most playlike of climbing practices. There is a climber, a rock, and their interaction. The natural environment also plays a fundamental role in my climbing. I think that climbing in general is a fantastic way to become aware of the richness of our planet and ideally learn to respect it.

MOVING WELL

To boulder successfully is to move well, which might be described simply as what works to solve the problem and get you up the rock. Yet, as you begin to move up the scale of difficulty, the movement possibilities become more limited. Climbing well means finding the most effective and efficient sequence of positions and transitions that can be achieved.

Climbing well is the efficient and imaginative meeting of mind, body, and rock. We can look at climbing not as a divisible series of steps but as a fluid transfer of energy from one point of balance to the next. Balance is essential so that the body uses the least effort to maintain position and resist gravity. The best climber is the one who constantly approaches balance regardless of position or direction of movement and is able therefore to use her energy productively and conserve energy. Poor climbing technique wastes energy and its repetition only trains the climber in doing the wrong thing.

The aim of climbing is to make the shape of the human body adapt to the shapes of nature. Climbers often think in terms of hand movements and sequences when they remember a climb. As a beginning tactic, this makes a great deal of sense. Because bouldering happens in a three-dimensional environment and includes the factors of time and energy, a more holistic approach is mandatory. For example, compression-type movements, where the climber relies on squeezing large features, are essential not just for V15 but much lower level problems in many areas today. To boulder at your best requires thinking not just in terms of individual points of contact or segments of the body or body stances. Good bouldering is an awareness of how to consciously integrate all of this and more, to the degree that it becomes a natural and unconscious gesture.

HANDHOLD TYPES AND GRIP POSITIONS

Climbing is often about hanging on, especially on steeper problems, and boulderers devote a lot of time to thinking about handholds. Your grip on the hold often depends on the type of hold. The more this knowledge becomes intuitive, the more quickly you can grab and use holds with less effort. To get started, let's look at basic types of holds you may encounter and how to use them.

EDGES

Edges are holds, usually horizontally oriented, that are incut, flat, or slightly sloping. They are often the width of two finger pads, or less, deep. There are three ways to grip an edge. When crimping, your fingers

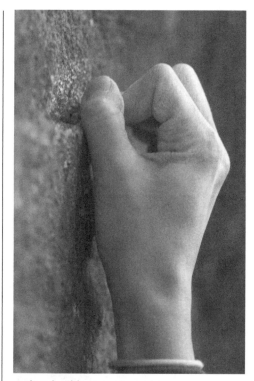

A thumb adds power to a crimp.
(Photo by Andy Mann)

are closed over a hold bent more or less at a 90-degree position at the first joint, often with your thumb against your forefinger, and your wrist bent back for leverage. This forms a kind of compression hook over a hold and can be extraordinarily powerful. The semicrimp is a less arduous and angled variation on the *crimp*. The thumb may be on another part of the hold.

The third way to grip edges is the open-hand position. In this position, the fingers are barely bent and mostly at the last joint,

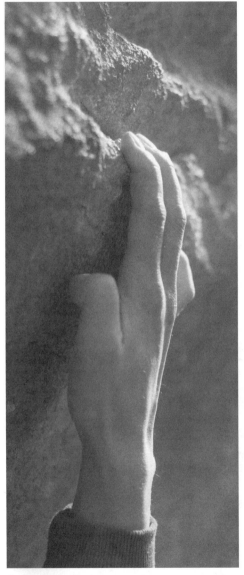

An open-hand grip on an edge
(Photo by Andy Mann)

the fingertip. The thumb may not play a role at all. This grip is also powerful and has a far lower risk of injury than the crimp, owing to the more neutral position of hands and wrist.

Holding onto small incut edges is a classic challenge on many boulder problems, but larger, less incut edges can also be challenging, especially on a very steep wall. Less defined edges require a whole body approach that focuses on opposition, where the weight of the climber against the hold makes the hold workable.

The best climber is the one who can adapt his grip and body position to make the most of the wide variety of holds on natural rock. Hard crimping, while a mandatory skill for many bouldering situations, requires a type of strength that can be limiting. Many hard problems involve sloping edges or pinches at some point and rarely feature textbook incut crimps. To give your forearms a break and balance your body's strengths, seek out irregular and difficult-to-use holds that require hard pulling from your core and legs, not just your forearms.

Beginning climbers do whatever comes naturally when they get started and this often means crimping. Crimping is the strongest grip used in climbing, but it is also the most injury-prone hand position. The raised knuckles exert terrific forces on the tendons in your fingers, increasing the likelihood of strain or tearing.

The open-hand position, which has fingers flat or extended, is a safer option for edges, and savvy boulderers use it whenever possible.

ANATOMY OF A HOLD: TO CRIMP OR NOT TO CRIMP

On this first move on a V11/12 boulder called *Clear Blue Skies* at Mount Evans in Colorado, I am using a crimp position for my right hand and snagging the first hold in an open-hand position. The next move involves a powerful and somewhat awkward cross to another edge for my right hand. The open-hand position's primary weakness is lack of leverage. It's hard to gain height from it. For the next move to work, I have to shift from an open-hand to a crimping position, building up enough body tension to make the next move. I find I often will make this transition in the course of a move, starting open-handed and then crimping to gain height. A clear example is seen in these photos of

Grabbing the terrible crimp on Clear Blue Skies *with an open-hand grip*

Jimmy Webb climbing the notoriously crimpy *European Human Being* (V12) in Chaos Canyon in Rocky Mountain National Park. He begins a powerful reach to a crimp in the open-hand position with the tips of three fingers grabbing the hold.

Jimmy Webb nabs a really bad crimp open-handed.

After getting good contact, Jimmy sets up in a full crimp for the last move. A full crimp helps gain the necessary distance to the obvious left hold he is aiming for. It also helps resist the *barn-door* swinging effect that this move produces as the climber's center of gravity shifts to the left.

Jimmy converts to a closed crimp position for the last hard move.

Another option is an intermediate position between the two extremes of full crimp and open-hand. This can be seen in this photo of my setting up the last move on *Clear Blue Skies*.

Setting up for the last move on Clear Blue Skies *(V12) at Mount Evans, Colorado*

The last move on this problem is a fairly powerful *dyno* off a poor left edge. The right hand is better but stays low. And, in order to set up for the move, I will first need to move my right foot up. An intermediate position allows me to minimize effort while hanging on to reset my feet and also allows a quick transition to the full crimp position for the final throw.

Sometimes part of the difficulty in a problem is mastering the exact position of your hand on a given hold and potentially needing to transition through different grip positions as you move. Often you will find yourself doing unlikely things such as crimping a *sloper* or open-handing a severely incut small edge. Find what works best for you and don't hesitate to try all alternatives. Even just an inch of height gained can mean success in finishing a boulder problem, so find the grip that lets you attain that extra height. But don't forget the dangers of intense full crimping. The power it offers can come with a high cost. Be careful.

UNDERCLINGS

Underclings are any kind of hold that you pull up from underneath. Underclings can be huge flakes on which you lean way out to reach high or small edges on which you have to rely on balance as much as power. Some holds, such as round pockets, may

An effective use of an incut undercling
(Photo by Andy Mann)

start as sidepulls and wind up as underclings as you move higher. Underclinging on steeper walls requires strong biceps but not only that: Balance, body position, and finger strength are important for underclings. Placing your legs and feet precisely and pushing off from them provides the oppositional leverage that makes underclings work.

SIDEPULLS

The sidepull comes in many different configurations, but they are all vertically aligned holds, and the climber pulls out on them perpendicular to the fall-line. They can be small and incut or broad and sloping, and their most useful feature is the way they can maximize your reach, especially compared to horizontal edges. Sidepulls are typically held in a thumbs-up position and work best in opposition to a decent foothold. Many boulder problems consist of moves between sidepulls, shifting weight to the left and right as needed. When the thumb can find purchase, pinched sidepulls are often more secure. They are also strenuous. It is almost always best to move through a sidepull as quickly as possible.

Sidepulls are especially strenuous when they are close to the body's center, say, right under the belly, limiting the opposition that can be generated. When using sidepulls, it is usually best to stay well off to the side of the hold and look for oppositional footholds. For example, a well-placed heel hook can help secure a poor sidepull. Sidepulls are also prone to the barn-door effect when the climber, having failed to secure a foothold

Sometimes you can discover very small wrinkles, seams, or crystals that allow a better grip on slopers. Some slopers are only climbable when the texture of the rock is pristine; that is, in cool, dry weather when the climber's hands aren't sweating and the hold is thoroughly cleaned of chalk or

A sharp, thin sidepull crimp (Photo by Andy Mann)

Effective position and skin contact is crucial with slopers. (Photo by Andy Mann)

on the opposite wall to counterbalance the sidepull, loses balance and is swung by gravity away from the hold: the body the door, the handhold the hinge.

SLOPING HOLDS

Slopers are hard-to-grip holds that are gently rounded or that slope away from the rock. They present a special challenge to the climber in that even slight adjustments in body position can make a huge difference to how useful they are. Effective use of footholds, the appropriate use of heel hooks, and core strength are generally key to making sloping holds work. Constant application of force is essential on this kind of hold, or you will lose contact and friction rapidly.

grease. At Fontainebleau in France, home to the notorious *plat*, an absurdly featureless sloping sandstone hold, certain problems are simply unclimbable before November or later than March or April, when the weather becomes too hot and humid. Similar issues are found at sandstone areas in the southern United States such as Horse Pens 40 in Alabama.

PINCH GRIPS

The power and versatility of the opposable thumb comes into play on an amazing variety of holds, and in bouldering, just

Pinching a big pebble (Photo by Andy Mann)

about every hold to one degree or another can be considered a pinch hold. Adding the use of your thumb can turn a poor hold into a much better one.

In a pure pinch grip, the fingers are on one side of a hold and the thumb on the other. It's a squeezing kind of grip that must be active to work well on most sloping holds. Hand size also makes a difference for pinch grips. Holds lending themselves best to pinch grips are horizontal fins, under-clings, and sidepulls. Especially for these, placing other limbs in opposition is crucial to getting the most out of the hold.

Pinch grips also require good choice and use of supportive footholds. The better you can place your feet, the more you can push and lessen the need to pull with the hands. Pinch grips, or pinches, are commonly encountered in gyms where the majority of holds offer some use of the thumb and many problems are set as primarily pinch-type moves. Success on these problems requires healthy amounts of power, dynamic movement, and accurate placement of feet and hands.

GASTONS

The move called the *gaston* is as much about body position as grip. These are holds that are grabbed in a reverse sidepull position, pulling toward your body with your thumb down. Usually gastons are a standing hold, oriented vertically to the ground and if the feet are well positioned can allow a surprisingly long reach. Gastons also are tough on your shoulders, stressing them in a particularly dangerous way. Especially

POCKETS

The action of water and wind erodes depressions in the rock, creating pockets, particularly in sedimentary rocks such as limestone, sandstone, and volcanic rock. The tuff found in Bishop, California, is one example but they can occur wherever the composition of the rock allows them to get started, including weaknesses in granite or gneiss.

In bouldering, pockets often present a real challenge, especially on harder problems, because they tend to isolate the

The burly second move on No More Greener Grasses *(V12) involves a hard gaston.*

dangerous are long reaches to gaston-type holds, whether to the side, above the head, or both.

A good three-finger pocket (Photo by Andy Mann)

Which one to use? (Photo by Andrew Burr)

rests, for example, on boulders in places like Hueco Tanks where gigantic pockets, or huecos, punctuate even the steepest walls. Encountering these kinds of holds can be a full-body experience, especially if they are sloping in any way.

CRACKS

Cracks are rock features that are a staple of roped climbing throughout the world, offering climbing possibilities and protection at the same time. Except on granite boulders, cracks are not commonly used in bouldering, but crack climbing skills are helpful in a number of non-crack situations. Crack climbing is usually called jamming and works through carefully inserting and twisting fingers, hands, and feet to lock them down in appropriate locations.

Finger jams are fairly common and work by placing the hand thumbs-up or thumbs-down in a spot in the crack that narrows down or pinches off. Thumbs-up jams work

fingers and minimize the help of the thumb in using them. This position exerts high levels of stress on the joints and tendons, making serious injury a real possibility, especially with one-finger or *two-finger* pockets. Whenever possible, it is best to grip pockets using an open-hand grip and beware of loading the hold too heavily, especially in dynamic movement. For pockets, hold-specific training can pay real dividends if done carefully.

Bigger pockets offer interesting possibilities for movement, including hand-foot matching, heelhooking, and even full-body

A thumbs-down finger jam can be painful but very secure. (Photo by Andy Mann)

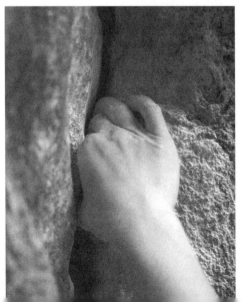

much like sidepulls (albeit more painful to the climber), allowing fairly secure, long reaches. Thumbs-down jams rely on twisting and torquing, making them—like gastons—even more painful on both fingers and shoulders.

Cracks vary in size, from wide fingers to hands, off-hands, fists, and off-widths, as more and more flesh is inserted into them. Success with these kinds of cracks may well depend on individual hand and body size as much as anything else. Hand jams are a particularly secure kind of jam, but for those climbers whose hands are too small or large for the crack, the jam may prove almost impossible to stick. Fist jams and off-widths are particularly difficult to negotiate, relying on a combination of strength, technical awareness, and sheer determination to succeed. Using cracks is not always as intuitive as using face climbing holds, especially to those just learning to climb, yet becoming experienced in crack holds allows access to amazing problems and routes.

Another aspect of crack climbing that is helpful to master is liebacking. Here the climber pulls on one side of the crack and pushes her feet against the other, staying in place through opposition and judicious use of footholds. Liebacking is a staple of traditional climbing, which emphasizes following natural features such as cracks, flakes, or inside corners. Often, boulder problems will offer similar features, though usually they are much shorter. The key to liebacking well is strongly pushing with the feet and confident, continuous movement. Liebacking is very strenuous if done

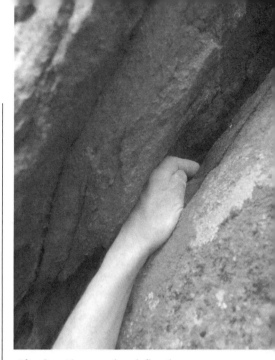

After inserting your hand, flex the area around your thumb to secure the jam.

poorly or without using footholds. As with sidepulls, savvy use of the feet and awareness of body position can make this kind of movement fun and secure.

KNOBS, SPIKES, AND HORNS

While much more common in a climbing gym, knobs are encountered outdoors as well, especially on conglomerate rock or granite. Bouldering areas such as Tuolomne Meadows at Yosemite have literally hundreds of them on the boulders. Knobs are distinct protrusions which can be grabbed with the whole hand and can be very useful in many ways, such as finishing jugs (knobs at the top of boulder problems), underclings, or highstep holds.

A classic grip for knobs is the hamhock position: The climber wraps his entire hand over the hold, usually with the thumb pointing down. Smaller knobs might be crimped or pinched. On natural boulders, it is very important to confirm the integrity of the hold before committing to it as knobs are vulnerable to breaking.

GYM HOLDS

The variety of holds produced by nature is infinite. In recent years, the variety of artificial holds produced by manufacturers has grown at an astounding rate. Earlier gym holds tended to imitate natural rock, but in recent years they resemble works of avant-garde sculpture, and are made from casts of golf balls and lightbulbs, to name a few examples. Instead of the smaller incuts and pockets typical of the 1990s, contemporary holds tend to be large, smoother, and more sloping: tricky stuff.

For climbers this is welcome news. The new surfaces and shapes are easier on the fingers yet still build strength and versatility. That said, some problems with gym holds must be recognized and acknowledged, especially with respect to climbing outside. Gym holds almost always allow engagement of the thumb, meaning that virtually every gym hold becomes a pinch grip. Once you are used to this, translating to outside rock can be a shock since thumb catches aren't always there. Also, gym holds always project out and away from the wall, creating positions and balance points often missing outdoors. Much the same goes for footwork, since outside many natural footholds do not allow the room for movement you can get in the gym. Finally, gym holds are usually much bigger and smoother than holds outside. If you are used to climbing

A typical section of wall at a climbing gym

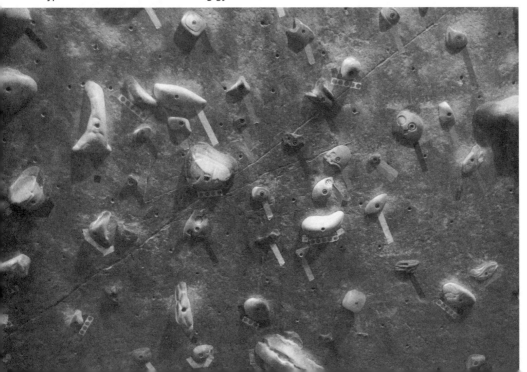

V5 on big slopers, an encounter with a sharply crystalled, crimpy V5 on rough rock may be surprising.

Climbing holds have become much more sophisticated than when they were first introduced, and today the best hold designers are creating subtle shapes, which demand thought, not just strength, to use well. If you plan to transition to natural rock, make sure you spend time in the gym on artificial holds that more closely mimic what you will find bouldering outside.

FOOTHOLDS AND FOOTWORK

Capable footwork is essential to good bouldering. Your climbing will improve greatly as you become better able to transmit force to your feet. The ability to readily transfer weight to the stronger muscles of your legs and core will translate into more efficient use of your fingers and arms, increasing the level of difficulty you can achieve as a climber.

In practice many factors affect good footwork, including the angle of the wall, quality and shape of foothold, and distance to the next handhold or between footholds. The degree to which a climber can consciously find ways to increase the load on her feet, even by a barely perceptible amount, is often the key to success on a difficult move. Maintaining contact with a foothold might mean achieving that really long reach between two bad handholds without swinging out or levering off the wall. Even the ability to push effectively

from your feet into a foot-free dynamic lunge can make a huge difference in terms of efficiency and distance. Also, transferring even a small amount of the total load away from the fingers and arms to the feet can enhance your chances of recovery and make success on the rest of the moves much more likely.

Perfect your ability to identify and use footholds quickly, even when they're out of sight. The more quickly you can locate a foothold, the better you can weight it and do the next move. You will want to develop a spatial awareness that allows you to relocate a feature made invisible or obscure by a change in position. A partner can point to crucial features, but on most boulder problems it is faster to find footholds yourself.

EDGING

The horizontal edge is the classic foothold and the easiest to use; however it presents its own unique challenges, especially when the edge is small or irregular. Some edges may literally be the thickness of a credit card and may be almost impossible to see, let alone use. A good edging shoe really pays off here, as well as strong calf muscles; but most important of all is a sense of balance and conviction that your foot, once placed, will stay.

On steep problems, the climber cannot simply stand on an edge but must pull down and out and will need to adjust to the ways in which gravity and weight interact on a given foot placement. As you practice this, you will develop a subconscious, almost automatic, response. This need for

A good foothold on an edge
(Photo by Andy Mann)

Sometimes an edge is so thin that smearing is the best way to use it. *Smedging*, or smearing an edge, means placing your toe just above the edge and pressing the shoe rubber into the edge at an angle so that you are not lining up the shoe edge with the hold so much as grinding the sole onto it.

The key to using smears is an intimate understanding of the hold and the friction it offers, perhaps down even to a few crucial crystals. A sensitive shoe is really helpful for smearing, as are strong feet, and strong fingers on the supporting handholds.

touch sensitivity is why most boulderers favor a more flexible and sensitive shoe that allows an immediate feel for the shape and size of a hold. Strong calf and foot muscles help maximize use of a hold. Levering your hips in close to the wall delivers more force to the foothold, pushing out as well as down, and allows more control of the upper body through the move.

SMEARING

Smearing, gaining the most shoe surface area possible on the rock, is one of the most important skills any boulderer can develop. Smears can be made at any angle. By definition, smearing requires active pressure and even so, can be thwarted by weather, rain, or lichen on the rock. The cleanliness of the hold or shoes and the climber's overall body position make a huge difference to a successful smear.

For an effective smear, you want a lowered heel, sensitive shoes, and patience.

CAMMING POSITIONS: KNEEBARS, KNEESCUMS, AND FOOT CAMS

In earlier climbing manuals, especially those written before 2000, use of parts of the body other than toes and fingers was underemphasized. Climbing developed at a sport-climbing area near Rifle, Colorado, radically changed this. Rifle has a number of outrageously steep walls festooned with a bewildering range of obtuse, blocky features. Classic crimp ladders or pocketed walls are rare here. To be able to climb well at areas like Rifle requires the development of skills such as kneebarring and foot camming.

Kneebars and scums. In their most typical form, kneebars require a foothold and an opposing feature at just the right distance so that when the climber places her foot, she can press the top of her upper leg, somewhere between the knee and mid-thigh on the opposing feature. To effectively use this position requires leaning out a bit so that the natural desire for the leg to straighten jams the knee and upper leg more securely in place. In its most secure form, the hands can be taken off entirely. In bouldering such scenarios are few, yet certain well-known problems are famous for requiring effective kneebars or at least kneescums.

Shannon's left knee supports her while she makes the next reach.

Bush Pilot, a classic V11 boulder problem in Rocky Mountain National Park, ascends a radically leaning, left-facing corner with scant actual holds. A well-set kneebar can ease some of the difficulty here. There is a story about a V11 problem called *The Feather* in Hueco Tanks that was tried without success until Fred Nicole used an obvious kneebar in a large *hueco* to get through the *crux*.

In bouldering, kneebarring allows a climber to use really poor handholds on a steep wall by keeping an active opposition in place until moving to more incut grips. At this point the kneebar is released and the climber swings out and re-establishes her feet on the wall. On really complex problems, that kneebar might be replaced by a heel or toe hook or another kneebar, and the problem might consist of many subtle adjustments around a single pair of poor handholds.

Foot cams. Another newly popular camming position involves the feet. Here the climber presses her heel on a hold and the top of the same foot into an opposing surface. This could be between two holds, in a horizontal crack, or within a large hueco.

Foot cams can be an extraordinarily effective way of extending your reach on a very steep wall, finding a way to rest, or using very poor handholds, much like kneebarring. This position demands caution and attentive spotting. If the cam is really good but the hands are really bad, the climber risks a heads-down fall with the cammed foot jammed in place, risking serious head injury or major knee or ankle damage.

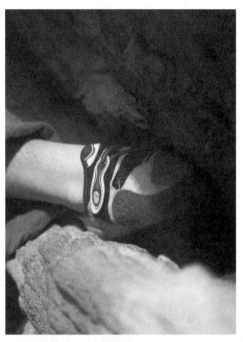

A heel-toe cam can hold you in when it's steep. (Photo by Andy Mann)

Any climbing position where the climber's back is close to horizontal is potentially hazardous because of the potential to hit the spine, neck, or head in a fall. Caution is also needed in any position where a body part is jammed in place. Be aware at all times of these hazards and plan accordingly.

HEEL HOOKS, TOE HOOKS, AND BICYCLING

If there is one technique that really shows the evolution of modern bouldering, it is the heel hook. Books, magazines, and videos before 2000 often show boulderers in a frontal position, fingers on crimps, toes on the holds, hanging away from the wall. With the turn of the millennium, a new climbing shape emerged. The climber is close to the rock, with a heel (or two) plastered to flat surfaces and the body compressed and curved, hugging sloping features rather than definable holds.

Heel hook. It is important to remember that heelhooking is not a passive position. In instances when the heel may be placed on nothing but a poor smear, a small edge

A good heel hook on a sloping shelf (Photo by Andy Mann)

or crystal, or in a position that prohibits an effective grip, the climber must really work to keep that heel in place. This is made especially difficult when you have to move from the heel hook since a slight shift in orientation can alter the effectiveness of the hold.

In the modern bouldering idiom, heel-hooking depends on opposition. Typically this will be against the opposite hand or the opposite foot. Often you must rotate the knee and foot so that the sole of your shoe is parallel to the wall and you are contracting simultaneously down and in toward your core. Your foot will be at waist or shoulder height to start. As you gain height on the heel hook, you will begin to turn your lower leg and foot downward, orienting your shoe sole toward the ground and beginning to *rockover*, but still always pulling in.

The heel hook is potentially quite hazardous to your knees, knee ligaments, and hamstrings, and most dedicated boulderers have at least strained a hamstring while heelhooking. Develop as much strength and flexibility in your lower body as you can, and learn to listen closely to your body as you try moves of this type. Do not push it too far. A torn hamstring takes a long time to heal and torn knee ligaments may never fully recover, even after surgery.

Toe hook. Another effective technique on steep terrain is a toe hook. An opposition technique, the toe hook allows greater extension of the body on terrain where no good incut footholds can be found. A typical situation would be a climber reaching very

Chris Schulte working a project (Photo by Andy Mann)

far to a reasonable hold and realizing that as soon as she lets go of the lower handhold, she will swing into space and fall off. If there is a feature on the wall facing away— the more like an undercling, the better— she can let go of a foot, situate the top of it up against the feature and pull hard upward with her toes, quadriceps, and abdominal muscles. Once the toe hook is secure, she lets go of the previous hand and resets it on another hold.

Toe hooks can be used with other toe hooks, heel hooks, kneebars, and conventional footholds. Bouldering shoes with plenty of rubber on top of the foot and at the heel will help with this.

One use of toe hooks commonly seen on large roof features is swinging out to a sloping lip with one or both feet and then matching the foot with a hand. Once the climber is more or less stable in this position, she can reset and move again. For example, often the toe hook is then switched to a heel hook to set up a mantel to top out the problem.

Bicycling. Occasionally a projecting feature or pair of features allows simultaneous toehooking with one foot and toe pushing with the other, working in tandem on the features. This is called bicycling and can allow surprisingly effective use of unpromising handholds. The key to

Toe hooks allow good opposition between the hands and feet. (Photo by Andy Mann)

Toehooking on Dark Waters *(V13), Clear Creek Canyon, Colorado* (Photo by Caroline Treadway)

A bicycle move holds the climber in position on an overhang. (Photo by Andy Mann)

all these techniques is an open mind and strong core muscles along with a capacity to rapidly predict how future movements will alter the overall distribution of weight.

Weighting the feet effectively is always a crucial step to doing any difficult move in bouldering. As we've seen, this can require unlikely and unobvious body positions and situations. The good climber is always looking for these kinds of solutions as they can save finger strength for other moves.

BODY POSITIONS

Your weight as a climber is managed more effectively when your torso is placed properly. In bouldering that means transferring weight to the feet whenever possible and keeping the whole body as much in balance as possible. Climbing is always about movement between body positions, and especially in bouldering, where stopping

to place or clip protection is unnecessary, maintaining continuity and momentum is essential.

UPPER BODY POSITIONS AND MOVEMENT

A typical beginning climber will climb in a straight-on, frontal position, meeting the wall square and keeping the chest high and body upright. In some climbing situations, especially on a wall that is about 75 degrees steep with secure, regular holds like a ladder, this position is appropriate. Yet in bouldering this situation is relatively rare and it doesn't offer very interesting climbing. More typical to bouldering are angles at or beyond vertical, often well beyond vertical, with holds and surfaces at an infinite variety of angles and orientations. When this terrain is encountered, tall, frontal approaches do not usually work well.

Given a climb that is past vertical or overhanging with handholds that are positive and incut, a relaxed, hanging position is best. This keeps your center of gravity low and the weight on your feet. Using straight arms transfers weight onto bone and tendons rather than muscle, conserving energy. Keeping your body positioned out away from the rock allows you to see handholds and footholds more clearly. As the handholds become more tenuous and father apart, you will be unable to maintain this loose attitude and stance and will have to rely on tension and compression to stay on the problem.

Twisting the hip. Twisting your hip and shoulder into the wall is a body position that pulls your center of gravity in close and forces your legs to push harder on the footholds. This can gain precious inches on a long reach and help maintain contact with the rock on poor or sloping holds. As the climbing intensifies, it is generally more effective to stay pulled in close to the wall since the tension from such a position allows better contact for the feet and hands.

Opposition. The upper body has to maintain opposition between handholds as well. In fact a number of problems consist of nothing but maintaining opposing forces between large sloping holds for hands and feet. Drawing upon the large muscles in your back and chest, as well as the abdominal muscles, is key here, all the while maintaining a constant state of tension to stay attached to the climb. This can be exhausting work, yet using better technique, breathing steadily, and finding miniscule opportunities to relax can pay huge dividends.

A stem across a corner

Balancing the need to stay attached and the need to move is at the heart of the sport of climbing. Here the boulderer has to consciously find the range where he can let go enough to generate the force that will allow progress. A static position is not

Ferdinand Schulte uses complex oppositional techniques to get up Bierstadt (V9/10) at Mount Evans, Colorado.

enough to actually make progress and in fact hinders it considerably. Dropping the hips a bit, letting the shoulders move out away from the wall just a little, bending the knees, all the while maintaining sufficient tension in the core; these movements must be learned through experience best directed by remembering that balanced movement is the ideal goal, even in the middle of strenuous, off-balance climbing.

Crossthroughs. Crossing through or crossing over (and under) is a very useful upper body position that can save a great deal of energy on moves that traverse or move across a wall. Here the climber reaches over the adjacent hand and twists into a position that allows a clean transfer of weight to the new hold. Sometimes these crossthrough moves are so extreme that the climber winds up facing away from the wall, a move that is sometimes seen in bouldering competitions and often called

A crossthrough (Photo by Andy Mann)

The rose move is rarely needed but it's an elegant traversing technique.
(Photo by Andy Mann)

a *rose move*. The essential element of successful crossthroughs is keeping your hips in close to the wall, rotating up and in along with the leading shoulder. You may start the move with a high right hip on a backstep to move the right hand up and left, and then, having gained the next handhold, switch feet and pull hard with the left hip to release the left hand to move up again.

Figure-4. This position is used in indoor competition climbing and was first recognized and adopted in the early 1990s as a means to reach up and onto a steep roof without the use of feet. For example, you might have a really good *jug* with your right hand and a hold well down on the same side for your left hand, yet you want to reach up and left. You begin by threading your left leg over your right arm so that the inside of your knee is resting on the inside of your elbow. Letting your center of gravity settle into place, you should then be able to let go with the left and reach

A competitor uses a figure-4 move in the Vail World Cup. (Photo by Jackie Hueftle)

statically for the next hold. A figure-4 is a very specialized technique; a well-executed dynamic move is almost always used instead, especially when climbing outside.

Manteling. The technique of manteling is often used to top out on a boulder that has no positive holds on top of it. Sometimes, boulderers will get to the lip of a hard overhanging problem and be unable to complete it because they are poorly versed in this very important maneuver. The essence of manteling is getting your hips and shoulders high enough and balanced enough to allow you to bring your foot up onto the top of a boulder or ledge and stand up on it. The most difficult part of manteling for many is finding this balance point from a very strenuous and precarious position near the top of a problem.

Pushing and balance are the key to good manteling technique.

The easiest kind of mantel is to arrive at the top of a vertical wall which ends in a broad and flat, horizontal shelf or ledge. Simply pull then push up onto both hands quickly, shifting one or both to a palm-down fingers-out position, so that your hips are above the lip. Put one foot over the lip (if the lip is level, it shouldn't matter which one) and shift your weight onto that foot. Press hard on that foot and keep moving up while pushing down with the opposite hand. At some point you will feel yourself naturally coming into balance over that foot to stand up fully.

Manteling is made much easier by features at the top that provide a handhold, so you are not relying solely on friction and balance. Look carefully for them as they can add a huge measure of security and lower the difficulty of that move. Even a small wrinkle or divot can be leveraged in this way, easing the climber's passage considerably.

A much more difficult situation is where the wall below the mantel is overhung and the slab above is low angle. These kinds of exits are complex, precarious, and potentially dangerous as the climber can easily lose balance and fall awkwardly and out of control. Awareness of body position and a good range of flexibility in the legs and torso are necessary. A well-managed landing area and a practiced spotter can be helpful as well.

To begin, assume you are *matching* hands (replacing one hand with the other on the same hold) at the top of a boulder, trying to get onto the low-angle slab above.

Pressing out a mantel (Photo by Andrew Burr)

You first have to decide which foot is going to lead. This is usually indicated by the angle of the lip; if it slopes down and left, the left foot should lead, and vice versa. Assume a left foot for this example. Pull in and up a bit and place a high left heel hook over the lip, keeping your foot pointed away and pulling in hard. Next you must try to raise your hips over the lip, trying to get your left knee pointing more to the left and moving your torso in closer to the rock. At some point you will feel the possibility of shifting your hand backward toward the lip, so that your weight is on your palm and your fingers are pointing down toward the ground, not up. Continue pushing with this hand until both hips are above the lip while keeping your shoulders low and close to the rock. Your head will probably be facing down and away from your foot, also in pretty close to the wall.

Next, shift your weight more and more onto the foot, continuing to push with the right hand. At some point you may feel able to release the left hand and find another hold higher to let you stand up. If no hold is available, keep working the foot, trying to get your hips over it until you can press into a standing position. To do this well requires strong thigh muscles, a great sense of balance, as well as a real faith in your ability to complete the move. At some point, you may not be able to reverse or bail out in a controlled manner so following through is crucial here.

Because manteling is often found at the top of a boulder, it is smart to practice this move on more friendly terrain, using features close to the ground that have good landings. A smooth and relaxed manteling technique can pay huge dividends in serious situation, so take some time to develop this skill, even though you may use it infrequently.

LOWER BODY POSITIONS

Understanding the ways in which the lower body can push you where you want to go is essential to making progress in bouldering. Don't assume that the upper body, especially arms and fingers, drives the act of climbing by pulling.

We find a stance that allows a hand to move only because we are holding weight with our feet. In other words, climbers are more like caterpillars, squirrels, and crawling babies, than like swinging monkeys. Enlisting the larger muscles in our legs and abdominal core to do the hard work of keeping our bodies on the wall is at the heart of better climbing form.

Stemming. Stemming is a simple position that allows even distribution of weight between two feet. In its classic form, stemming occurs in an inside corner or other recessed space where the climber can stand, feet on opposing holds, with practically no assistance from hands. In this kind of climbing, easy progress can be made by pressing alternately between both hands and both feet.

Some stems can involve opposition between hands and feet as in the famous problem *Stem Gem* in Joshua Tree National Park. A good sense of balance and friction is useful for successful stemming.

Stemming a corner is a great way to climb efficiently. (Photo by Andrew Burr)

Stemming is not confined to corners or chimneys. On any wall where the possibility of pressing between two footholds exists, the power of stemming can be put to work. A knob or pebble can provide a great rest if used in conjunction with another foothold on a vertical wall. Two small inset corners facing each other can allow much easier progress even on a very overhung face. The key is being able to rapidly recognize and use these kinds of features when they present themselves. Because stemming gives the fingers and arms good long rests, it should be a priority climbing skill to master.

Chuck Fryberger finds a stem in Baja, Mexico. (Photo by Andrew Burr)

Backstepping. One of the signs of a beginning climber is the constant use of the inside edge of the foot (the edge with the big toe) while climbing. While using the inside edge is important in all forms of climbing, it is also important to learn to use all parts of the foot and especially the outside edge. One of the most common uses for the outside edge is to step up and to the side for a hold, especially in conjunction with a sidepull.

Using the example of reaching up and right from a left sidepull, you might find yourself pulling your right hip in close to the wall as you turn to face the left, turning your right foot to point to the left as you step onto it using the outside edge of the right foot. Your left foot might be flagged off to the left, acting as a counterbalance, either using a small foothold to push with or simply smeared against the wall. In this position you will find yourself able to reach much farther and more securely than is typical for someone climbing pigeon-toed and using the foot's inside edge.

Backstepping is especially helpful on overhanging walls where the proximity of the hip turned to the wall means more weight transferred to the feet. The relatively passive position of the arms in this kind of move, combined with the focus of weight on the feet, allows use of even relatively poor holds on very steep walls to gain height. Backstepping is closely related to dropkneeing in this respect.

Dropknees. The dropknee is a more advanced climbing skill that combines aspects of stemming and backstepping. In essence it is a backstepped foot placed up closer to the hip and leveraged with an opposed foothold. The idea behind the dropknee is finding a hold that allows you to place a foot on it so that your toes and knee point down and twist away from

Here the outside edge of the right foot is supporting the climber's weight.

In addition to backstepping, dropknees are a huge help on hard moves.

the wall a bit. The other foot provides the opposition point. If both feet are reasonably secure, the climber can twist the hip away from the dropkneed foot and pull up and into the wall. This usually frees the hand on the same side as the dropknee to reach, often quite far.

The dropknee is a great technique for steep, crimpy faces with lots of possibilities for feet. Even steep roof features can be climbed with this technique. In the gym, many problems succumb to this kind of move. Yet do not rely too much on this technique for resolving difficult moves, since many harder problems do not offer the sort of footholds needed for the dropknee position. In addition, dropknees can present serious hazards to knees. The twisting and pressing motion is powerful enough to tear ligaments if done improperly and especially in the more extreme versions of this move.

Carlo Traversi uses a dropknee on The Dominator *(V13) in Yosemite.* (Photo by Jackie Hueftle)

Rockover. This lower body movement is one of the most useful techniques for completing boulder problems and making progress on lower angle walls. A rockover is when you are able to step high onto a foothold and move up enough to be able to sit on your foot and press up into a standing position, with minimal use of the hands. The key to a successful rockover is a good sense of balance and turnout of the hips.

Rockovers are often used in conjunction with heel hooks and mantels to ease transitions between steep overhangs and lower angle slabs. Injuries from highstepping and rockovers are common, however, and it is important not to stress the knee excessively in this kind of move. Because they focus on one foot, rockovers are often done in conjunction with flagging.

Flagging. Flagging refers to allowing one leg to be placed so that it is not on any particular hold, often totally hanging

A rockover can be an efficient way to reach higher.

A flagging move often follows a rockover.

Flagging keeps you in balance. (Photo by Caroline Treadway)

in space, while the other leg takes weight. Flagging is used to balance or counterbalance the body's weight over a foothold and often to stabilize the climber against a swing to one side or the other.

Purposely climbing with one foot off the wall seems to go against common sense, but flagging makes sense, especially in bouldering. A classic flag situation might be a climber wanting to reach to the right with only a high foothold on the left available. To do this move most easily would probably require rocking over the left foot and then letting the right leg extend to the left to find balance. By finding this balance point the climber can avoid swinging back to the left as the right hand moves up.

Another situation that is common arises with backstepping: for example, reaching up with the right hand with a backstepped right foot. The left leg is then extended to provide balance and to help match the center of gravity above the right foot. Pushing off even from a very small crystal or edge would then help maximize the reach of the flagged move.

Active flagging. Many instances of flagging can be relatively passive, used mostly for positioning the body more favorably for the next move by seeking a relaxed and natural balance point. Flagging can also take a more active, even dynamic role in propelling or kicking the climber into the move. This technique first saw major discussion in the mid-1990s as climbers noticed how Chris Sharma, then in his teens and sending everything in sight, tended to leave a leg off the wall and kick it up and back as he moved higher. This seemed counterintuitive to many as it appeared to remove a potentially useful foot. What Chris realized was that this foot and leg, freed from the wall, offered the possibility of adding momentum to a move that an attached foot could not. More recently this style of dynamic movement has been described as the *pogo*, but other names have been used as well.

For active flagging, imagine a scenario where you have two relatively poor holds for your hands and you want to go left with only a fairly high right foothold. The distance required is too far for a backstep and hip-twist lock-off and the right hold really isn't good enough to lock it off any way.

To use an active flag, you step up on the right foothold with the right foot, still keeping your hips low, forcing your right knee to bend a bit. Your left foot should be dangling, and a bit bent as well. Then you pull on both arms together, and while you are moving up, push down with the right foot

Leaning out with the right foot ready to help kick the climber up

The right foot is still kicking as the climber reaches for the next hold.

and actively straighten and kick the left leg up and left, driving your hips up and left. As the momentum builds, you can let go with the left hand and latch the next hold. One of the benefits of this technique is that your center of gravity rises up and out with the move and remains in a neutral position when you latch the hold, dampening some of the outward or sideways movement common in dynamic movement.

One of the drawbacks to active flagging is that in order to be successful it requires a strong degree of coordination as well as fingers, back, and biceps strength. And as always with dynamic moves, there is a real risk of injury from improper take-off or landing onto a hold.

Such momentum-oriented climbing emphasizes a high degree of kinetic awareness and requires a fair amount of practice to pull off consistently. Such movement can add speed and confidence to your climbing style, assets in the sport of bouldering. Decreasing dependence on relatively static moves is necessary for moving up the scale of difficulty in the sport of bouldering.

THE BIG PICTURE

We learn to boulder well by mastering climbing technique. This involves fusing the different body positions, holds, and movements into a unified whole.

GRAVITY

To begin to tie together upper and lower body in coherent, effective movement, you need to think about how the human body interacts with gravity, that inevitable attraction toward the earth that is both the foundation of the sport and the bane of the boulderer. To climb is to negotiate with gravity, since fighting gravity is a losing proposition. Yet with the correct application of energy, you can work with gravity and even make it work for you.

There is almost always some means by which your weight can be distributed or arranged to resist the pull of gravity and direct it to some more helpful path. Generally speaking, it is best to begin by considering the concentration of core body mass from the knees to the torso to the shoulders to the head. On lower angled walls, this mass can be directly loaded upon the muscles of the legs and feet, parts well adapted to heavy constant loads. Keeping one's knees bent and feet responsive to the holds and monitoring the balanced distribution of weight between the feet can solve virtually any difficulty up to about 80 degrees of steepness.

When you get much past 85 degrees, the torso begins naturally to lean out and away from the wall, and any progress requires leaning the body into space unless a recess of some kind permits a stemming position. The arms carry more weight and as the wall leans past vertical, the amount of body mass that can be supported by footholds begins to drop.

This is the terrain that boulderers often tackle, especially in the upper levels of difficulty. The challenge of steep climbing is to direct as much of that weight burden

Dave Graham on The Great War for Civilisation
(V13), Lincoln Lake, Colorado
(Photo by Caroline Treadway)

energy to maintain and inhibits free movement from one position to another. The climber needs the middle road between being too static and bound and too loose and unattached. Justen Sjong, elite free climber and climbing coach, notes, "An intuitive climber who's efficient can focus on bigger fish like the mental game. A sign of mastery is fluid as opposed to mechanical movement."

BODY'S CORE

Key to successful bouldering is an understanding of the body's core and the role of core strength in climbing. If I have given the impression that the upper body is a burden in climbing, nothing could be further from the truth. Without the stability provided by the central core, climbing could not occur. The muscles of the back and abdomen position the entire body and permit the movement of one limb and ensure the fixed position of the other. It is through the anchor of the core that the strength of the arms, hands, and feet channel energy and movement. The energy provided by a strong body core is inestimably valuable, and while boulderers often obsess about finger strength, for the powerful extended moves on steep terrain that bouldering requires, they should obsess about a strong core as well. Without core strength, the strongest of fingers are unable to perform at their peak.

It is the job of the boulderer to find creative ways to ensure that the core can do its job well. Jason Kehl notes, "A lot of climbers are more textbook, only asking,

to the legs and feet as possible. As we have seen, there are a number of specific techniques such as heel hooks, heel-toe cams, toe hooks, and kneebars that can achieve that task. But to apply those moves and techniques well also requires understanding their roles and their limitations.

The essence of the problem is that the body's core mass wants to swing out to be in line with the pull of gravity. Sometimes that free-hanging state is useful, but usually it is not. Nor is a static clinging posture on a steep wall, since it requires a great deal of

Kevin Jorgeson fights to stay on the Spectre *(V13), in Bishop, California.* (Photo by Andy Mann)

'Where's my right foot go?'; they're not really learning. Do what you think instinctually, that's where the creativity comes out."

DYNAMIC MOVEMENT

One of the most distinctive contributions that bouldering has made to other types of climbing is an acceptance of dynamic rapid movement. Traditional climbing, for much of its history, has consisted of a controlled, somewhat static style of climbing that emphasized safety and the ability to retreat if need be. But in the 1950s and 1960s, boulderers such as John Gill and Bob Williams saw the potential in using the momentum of a swift upward throw to complete moves previously regarded as impossible. Film footage shows Gill, honed in part through his gymnastics training, winding up to launch and land, almost floating and with remarkable precision, at the next handhold. Today, climbers have taken such ideas to incredible levels of refinement and skill. Contemporary bouldering revolves around dynamic movement.

The classic dynamic movement, or dyno, is a long move from one decent hold to another, a move so long that it is unrealistic for most people to try statically. In some cases, it may even entail letting go of the previous hold and swinging onto the next. There are many variations on the theme of dynamic movement that I will try to explain here, all of which can aid in solving a boulder problem.

TJ Kelly nailing the dyno on Rasta Drop *(V7), Poudre Canyon, Colorado* (Photo by Andy Mann)

There are a number of principles to understand from the beginning when learning to move dynamically. The first is that whenever possible the feet should be doing most of the work. The ability of your spring-loaded legs to propel you upward is much greater than that of your arms. Even a very small foothold can generate a great deal of force if used correctly. Being able to transmit force through the feet may make completion of a dyno more straightforward, especially if the feet can be kept on the holds. The arms are essential but primarily in guiding the movement of the climber.

Second, you must learn to control and channel this force accurately. The direction you need to follow may not necessarily be upward. It may be across, or out and across, or even down. This force must be transmitted through the entire sequence from initiation to landing and beyond. Dynoing is not a simple matter of throwing for a hold but a complex process of applying force.

Third, you must prepare yourself physically and even psychologically for this kind of movement. The forces generated in dynamic climbing can be quite severe, risking injury to fingers, wrists, and shoulders in sideways or upside-down falls. Psychological preparation means building the self-confidence that makes dynamic moves successful and safe instead of scary and ineffective.

Fourth, you must learn to recognize the power of the deadpoint. This is the point in the trajectory of an upwardly moving climber when the climber is just at the crest of the move, when, in essence, he is weightless and motionless. This is the place to be when grabbing the next hold. The ability to apply force in this instant makes it much easier to stay on the problem when momentum comes back into the picture on the way down.

Sticking the throw on Cage Free *(V11), Boulder Canyon, Colorado* (Photo by Caroline Treadway)

A typical scenario is a climber on a moderately overhung wall, hanging on two decent holds, looking at a hold several feet higher, with nothing in between to aid in moving up. The first thing to do is assess the next hold. Is it a big jug or a poor sloper? A thin crimp? A big jug means a sizeable margin of error and less need for control. A poor sloper calls for a careful sizing up of trajectory and angle and keeping body tension strong. If your feet cut loose here you will not easily stay on the sloping hold. A small crimp means using high precision and being ready to bail if you don't catch the hold correctly, in order to avoid injury. The same applies to small pockets. Do not try to hold a poorly executed dyno unless you really want to get injured.

Let's say it's a big jug, meant for a right-hand catch. Here you would find the highest reasonable position for your feet, and then leaning out on your feet, drop your hips low and straighten your arms. Your eyes are focused on the hold above. Next, pressing down on your feet and pushing with your legs, you push your hips high and move up on the handholds, keeping more of an outward pull as you move higher. As you feel yourself approaching the highpoint of the move, let go with your right hand and aim for the jug, grabbing it as you continue to push on your feet. You may even feel as though you are primarily standing on your feet as you finish the move.

While you're catching the next hold, your feet may cut away from the holds and the wall. It is best to go with the swing, trying to keep the lower hand on as you stabilize your

Double dynos are exciting and fun to land correctly.

upper body. You can dampen this kind of swing somewhat by doing a kind of leg lift as you rise up, using your stomach muscles to diminish the centripetal force. It may be more relaxing to let the momentum carry you a bit, maybe even into the next move since you are on a big hold. Resisting the swing may be more strenuous and counterproductive than relaxing and using it constructively.

Dynamic movement is not just about huge lunges and throws. Hard boulder problems often involve insecure, short moves between bad holds. Here precision and planning are key as you may want your fingertips to line up on very small crystals the first time you touch without slipping or shifting. Slipping, shifting, or releasing can cut skin, injure tendons, or just be a waste of time and energy. Here you may find it useful to go through the motions while standing on the ground, moving your hand and grabbing the hold as though you were executing the move. After five to ten successful rehearsals, try the move for real, confident that you will not waste valuable time (and flesh scraped on rock!) by making mistakes in aim and contact position.

The risk for injury is high in dynamic movement. Keep the odds in your favor through careful planning. Make sure your landing zone is a flat and obstacle-free surface. Make sure your spotters are competent and alert. Think through the implications of a missed or half-caught throw. Where will you wind up? Obstacles that seemed out of the way may be closer, given a big swing, than you think. Especially in the gym, be sure to clear the landing well; other climbers may not be as tuned in to the situation as they could be.

Be especially careful about completing any dyno. Poor or small holds can injure not just fingers but also shoulders and elbows, injuries that require months to heal and which, in the case of shoulder dislocations, can permanently weaken the joint. Even solidly sticking or attaining a good hold one-handed can badly strain a rotator cuff if mismanaged. Many very strong young boulderers have experienced debilitating injuries and long layoffs through dynos,

especially in competitions where such moves are routine. Rather than following through and pulling on your arm, for example, let go if the move is poorly executed. You can always try again but only if you stay uninjured.

COMPRESSION

Compression climbing relies on opposition and core strength. It is often used on defined features, like a long arête or corner, with few or no defined holds. The classic situation might be an overhanging, double-sided arête. In this example, the climber pulls hard with two hands to place a good heel hook with, say, a right foot, maybe even immediately next to the right hand. By squeezing really hard between the left hand and the right foot, he then moves the right hand a little higher to a slight divot. Now he takes the left foot and finds a small toe hook, pulls hard on this and the right hand, and is able to move the left hand to a small crease. Then he moves both feet, cutting loose for an instant, and finds heel hooks for both feet, before resetting a hand higher, and so on.

Such climbs require cool, dry conditions for skin and shoe rubber to work effectively. These problems are very physical, yet the climber must be in tune with subtle shifts in weight and balance, learning when to relax and when to pull harder. Because progress is so friction-dependent, falls can be sudden and hard, making groundfall injuries to the head and back more likely if landing zones are not thoroughly padded. For compression climbing, climbers must

Chris Schulte on the streamside classic Authentic Battle Damage *(V12), Boulder Canyon* (Photo by Andy Mann)

keep their legs (especially the hamstrings), lower back, and hips strong and flexible.

Increasingly more modern boulder problems fall into this category. Relatively blank, obtusely angled features are relatively common on granite boulders, for example. Adept use of compression climbing can often unlock seemingly impossible moves or sections of rock. Compression climbing is also popular in inside competition where large slopers and volume features create dramatic, crowd-pleasing difficult moves that demand major exertion and effort from climbers.

Mastering this style of climbing is important to become a skilled overall boulderer. It can also be rewarding to the climber to find that sweet spot in a heel or toe hook that transforms a frustrating sloper into a usable and even comfortable hold.

MOMENTUM AND TIMING

In the climbing big picture, momentum and timing are everything. If bouldering is about expending energy, it makes sense that moving more efficiently conserves energy for when you really need it. Momentum is a helpful tool in energy efficiency. When you really need it, go for it. As longtime boulderer and climbing author Matt Samet says, "Be mean, be fierce, and be ready to dyno: Make your 'Grrr Face' and *jump* for that next hold. Only trying harder than you ever thought possible will see you up your most difficult problems."

Many boulderers act as if they are a bit surprised to reach the next hold. They stop when they get there, look around a bit, shift their hands, maybe reset their feet and then think about the next move. Pauses and hesitations like this add up quickly on harder problems and can prevent success. More experienced boulderers don't stop but

Jamie Emerson looking for the lip on Small Arms, *Lincoln Lake, Colorado*
(Photo by Caroline Treadway)

maintain the flow move to move, stopping or slowing as little as possible and only where it makes sense to do so. Their vision constantly shifts forward, scanning the footholds and focusing on the next hand placement.

A good way to get momentum started is to understand fully the sequence of moves on the problem before you leave the ground. Locating the holds and likely sequences in advance and remembering the moves from previous attempts saves so much energy that really careful attention to this alone may boost your climbing ability a grade or two from the outset. This can be refined even to the degree of remembering finger positions, foot angles, and specific microfeatures of holds. By anticipating these small adjustments, you reduce the time and energy needed to find them, saving that energy for more important tasks.

By climbing steadily, you build more efficient movement patterns to apply to other problems and other sessions. These movement patterns build confidence and optimism, attitudes that can significantly reduce perceived difficulties.

Sometimes, however, you are forced to stop in order to adjust your position on a hold or to change direction. Sometimes you may need to rest or shake a hand to get a little energy back. Sometimes you will want to go faster or slower. Incorporating these changes into climbing progression is all part of pacing. Even on a relatively short problem, you may want to smoothly and quickly get to a hold, shake for a second, push hard into the crux, and then relax while climbing

to the end. On a longer problem, you may want to vary your pace so that the hard sections are done quickly and rests are taken at in-between holds and stances. Going all out all the time usually results in rapid onset of fatigue and the inability to focus mentally.

Being mindful of pace can also be helpful in a day of bouldering. Taking your time on the approach, warming up gradually, dialing in on the day's project, taking breaks, and knowing when to call it quits are all opportunities to recognize your most effective and appropriate pace. The more effective you are at pacing, the more productive and memorable the day is likely to be.

FLOW: CONSCIOUS AND UNCONSCIOUS AWARENESS

Psychologists have studied the phenomenon called flow ever since Mihály Csíkszentmihályi first published his groundbreaking 1990 book, *Flow: The Psychology of Optimal Experience*. This book was the first close study of a mental state experienced by musicians, artists, athletes, and other performers of difficult tasks, a state of total immersion and inner awareness where remarkable things are done with no perception of effort or difficulty.

A close study of the principles of flow shows a direct correlation with the practice of bouldering. The pairing of climber and problem in the right way, with skill and challenge both at their peak, with total understanding of the problem and its solution, and instant feedback in the event of success or failure; all these factors can promote a state of mind that is serene and

Saturday Night Live, a famous dyno at Joshua Tree, California (Photo by Andrew Burr)

even joyful in the midst of extraordinary physical and mental stress.

While much of bouldering involves effort, hard work, and physical discomfort, most boulderers can recall the moments when everything just seemed to fall into place perfectly, there was no need to think or worry, and success seemed inevitable. These moments are rare and valuable, and many boulderers will go months or years between them. Yet the remarkable thing about flow is that it is accessible at all levels of ability. Even a beginning climber can taste this experience of perfect union of effort and task and build upon it for future progress in the sport.

Flow is a state of heightened perception that allows unconscious thought and movement patterns to take over. Many describe, for example, altered perceptions of time that are elongated and slowed down. A good way to prepare for flow is to promote awareness of yourself and what you are doing at all times when climbing. Perceiving yourself, your situation, and your actions in as much detail as you can is a great way of beginning the process. Being open to alternatives and remaining curious and open-minded about possibilities for solving climbing moves also increases awareness.

Strive therefore to instill good natural body movement and think and feel with a clear mind. With repetition and practice of these bouldering movements, they become ingrained to the point of being automatic. With little need to consciously supervise your body, your mind is freer to perceive what is going on and relax, enabling ever more efficient and pleasurable climbing, even at the height of difficulty. In rare instances, you will feel yourself go on a kind of autopilot, where it seems as though someone or something else has just directed what you have done. That is the state of flow.

TYPES OF TERRAIN

Different sorts of rock features call for different moves so it's useful to know the type of terrain you'll be encountering. If the area you're visiting is known for its corners, for example, you'll want to brush up on your liebacking.

SLAB CLIMBING

Slab climbing refers to climbing walls between 70 and 85 degrees steep that have very few and small holds. The challenge of slab climbing lies in balance and friction. Some slabs will require pure friction, but others rely on dime-width footholds and handholds. The best slab climbers have an intuitive sense of how much weight a poor, smeary foothold will take and how to distribute overall body weight between feet and hands to best make progress.

The best climbing stance for slabs is a bit away from the wall with weight centered on the feet. But harder moves may require the climber to get in closer to the rock, especially as handholds worsen.

In all kinds of slab climbing, a high degree of patience and tolerance for very unlikely holds and positions is important. Persistence matters because you may not know if you will succeed doing a given move until it is over. Some holds are so small, slippery, or otherwise fickle that it seems almost a matter of luck as to whether you will stay on. Flexibility and hip turnout center the climber's weight over his feet. Strong legs turn a high step onto a poor foothold into a secure

Balance and footwork are the keys to good slab climbing. (Photo by Andrew Burr)

The immaculate V5 slab of the Agnes Vaille Boulder (Photo by Andy Mann)

rockover, even with no handholds available. Strong feet are required to keep shoes stable and responsive to poor footholds.

A great example of slab climbing in the United States is the notorious *Slim Pickins* in Hueco Tanks, Texas. In an area famed for steep walls and roofs littered with incut edges and huecos, this V5 is notorious for spitting off the unwary. Angled at about 80 degrees, it has mostly fingernail-sized holds and miserable footholds. Balance and a cool head are mandatory here.

When trying a difficult slab, make sure that your shoes are immaculately clean and that there is no extra chalk on the handholds or footholds. Dirt, chalk, even particles of shoe rubber on holds can interfere with friction. It goes without saying that hard slabs are best tried on cooler days when skin friction is at its best and shoe rubber performs best. For virtually all types of climbing, but especially for slabs, it's much harder to climb well with direct sun and warm temperatures.

CORNERS

Prominent features such as cracks, corners, and arêtes define classic lines for climbers of all types. The aesthetic appeal of the direct line is often matched by clean, athletic moves. Inside corners, also called dihedrals, diedres, or open-book corners, present good examples of such problems. An inside corner offers stemming, liebacking, or some combination of the two. Sometimes the corner begins after a few moves of face or slab climbing or will end below the top, presenting a serious manteling challenge.

If presented with an obvious crack in a corner, liebacking is usually the way to go. Leaning off the crack, working the feet, and moving quickly from *stance* to stance will pay the biggest dividends. Finding stemming rests and hanging straight-armed from the better holds saves energy.

CRACKS

Cracks come in all sorts of sizes and angles, and while they are not as common in bouldering as faces, roof, or arêtes, they feature in many classic boulder problems.

The slippery finger crack/seam of Seurat *(V8) at Mount Evans*

The final moves on Autobot *call for strenuous liebacking.*

Jamming a thin crack (Photo by Andrew Burr)

Unless the wall is very steep or the crack very bad, most crack problems tend to be relatively easy once you get the technique down. Learning how to use finger and hand jams is very helpful, as is recognizing when to lieback and when to stem.

ARÊTES

An arête is a feature defined by an outside corner where two planes of rock meet. An arête can be slabby, vertical, or overhung. They can be very sharp or relatively blunt or curved. One of the most important aspects of arête climbing is maintaining opposition between hands and feet on either side of the arête edge. Heel hooks and sidepulls are helpful as is a high level of commitment and precise technique. A good arête feature is perhaps the most striking kind of line in bouldering and always worth seeking out.

Isaac Caldiero working up a perfect arête in the Utah desert (Photo by Caroline Treadway)

Chris Schulte on a nice arête at Fontainebleau
(Photo by Jackie Hueftle)

ROOFS

Bouldering is often about seeking the hardest challenges, and very steep wall and roof problems are the usual haunt of the dedicated boulderer. Most climbers consider a roof to be a wall set at least 60 degrees beyond vertical, and usually closer to horizontal. These are among the most strenuous kinds of problems due to the reliance on the arms and fingers. Many roof problems rely on adept use of features and footholds to take some of the weight off. Looking out for heel hooks, toe hooks, bicycle moves, dropknees, or even kneebars can be crucial to making roof problems feasible. Sometimes rotating your body in space may be required, perhaps to place a toe hook out at the lip of a roof before reaching out to match feet and hands.

Kevin Jorgeson on the first ascent of Unshackled *(V10), Lincoln Lake, Colorado* (Photo by Andy Mann)

Kevin Jorgeson heading to the lip on the hard highball Evilution *(V12), Bishop, California* (Photo by Andy Mann)

A dynamic and confident climbing style is helpful for many roof situations but so is pacing, finding rests, and taking advantage of decent, shakeout holds. When climbing a hard roof problem, a good spotter and thorough pad coverage is essential for safe climbing. If a hand suddenly slips, the climber can fall headfirst or land hard on his back or tailbone.

OVERHANGING WALLS

Overhanging walls are the most common situation for most boulder problems of any advanced difficulty. These are planes of rock overhung at least 5 to 10 degrees past vertical. After about 50 degrees past vertical, it is more like a roof. The most straightforward problems might simply have a series of edges leading to an easy *topout*. However, even the flattest plane of rock might have surprises in store. Be prepared for underclings, sidepulls, pockets, pinches, dropknees, kneebars, toe hooks, and heel hooks, to name some of the holds and techniques needed.

Especially important are a good sense of balance and precise, powerful footwork. Bold, confident movement is always helpful in bouldering, but on overhanging walls, it is essential. Handholds may be far apart and height off the ground is gained quickly. Rapid, precise use of holds improves your chance of successes immeasurably.

ROCK TYPES

Learning about rock types adds a great deal to the bouldering experience. Bouldering areas offer a surprising variety of unique rock features and textures.

Volcanic rocks are the product of volcanic activity at the surface of the earth. Dark, smooth and often columnar, diorite and basalt are commonly encountered as the more flaky and pocketed tuff, which is made from volcanic ash.

Igneous rocks form from magma that has cooled well below the surface of the earth. A slower cooling process results in larger crystals, the sort that is common in many forms of granite. The rock at Hueco Tanks is made from another igneous rock, syenite.

Sedimentary rocks include limestone, made from the deposits of the skeletons of sea creatures; sandstone, the recemented byproduct of wind- and water-eroded rock; and conglomerate, identifiable by its large pebbles and pieces of gravel. Conglomerate can often have glass-shard sharp edges. Sandstone, some types softer and harder than others, is a very popular rock for bouldering.

The last major category of rock is metamorphic. Heat and pressure have altered these rocks from their original state.

Quartzite is a metamorphosed, hardened version of sandstone, while gneisses are usually reconstituted granites and schists. Both exhibit horizontal layers climbers find helpful. Gneiss, in particular, shows multiple folds and complex fracture patterns, making it a great bouldering medium, as seen in many of the rocks in Rocky Mountain National Park.

Once exposed, rock is sculpted by wind, water, and biological agents of change such as lichen and trees. Weaknesses in the rock fill with water, then freeze and thaw cycles inexorably split the rock, forming cracks and flakes, and eventually reducing the boulder to gravel. Water is also a mild solvent, dissolving minerals that cement crystals together, forming pockets, and deepening flakes. In limestone formations, huge caves can result and dripping calcite can form the distinctive ribs called *tufas*. Water in the form of glaciers also transports huge boulders great distances, leaving behind erratics, rocks that have wandered far from their origin point. Over millions of years these forces gradually shape and mold the rock into the playground we enjoy today.

Please do not add to the process by creating your own holds. Instead enjoy the awareness of deep geological time that these beautiful holds and formations represent.

CHAPTER 4

Lisa Rands bouldering near Stone Fort, Tennessee (Photo by Andrew Kornylak)

Tactics

This chapter addresses the movement and protection strategies needed for different bouldering situations. Lowballs, traverses, and highball bouldering each present different climbing challenges. Spotting, pad placement, landing preparation, topping out, downclimbing, descending, as well as rehearsal and cleaning tactics are described.

TY LANDMAN ON *NEW BASE LINE*

Ty Landman is one of the most impressive young climbers to emerge in recent years. After an intense year or two of climbing some of the hardest problems in Europe and the United States, Ty left the climbing scene to finish up college and see another side of life. I expect he'll be back.

I made my first trip to Magic Wood when I was twelve, and immediately liked it. I can remember wandering around the mossy forest, looking at the majestic boulders of perfect river granite, and finding *New Base Line* for the first time. Even though I didn't know of any of the problems, the line really stood out—the diagonal crack sloping to what seemed a blank finishing wall. Though of course in retrospect it was ridiculous, I sat and stared for a while, and then put my shoes on—totally oblivious to the situation. Minutes later my friend walked up the hill to tell me that I was standing under an 8B+ boulder. It was probably the first problem I walked away from, awaiting the day that I could climb it.

Five years passed during which I'd been on many short trips to Magic Wood. This trip I knew I was climbing well, but July is certainly the wrong time to climb in Magic, so hopes weren't too high. Having had a couple days on *New Base Line* over the last years, I felt confident that I could pull it out of the bag and move it into the satch. As 9:00 PM on July 21, 2008 came around it got colder, so my attempts came closer. As per usual we'd forgotten headlamps and the supermarket had closed; darkness was setting in and so was hunger. I decided to give a last ditch effort before racing to the pizzeria. At the *redpoint crux* I drilled my toe down and tried to keep tension. It felt good to be linking sections for the first time with success in reach. Thankfully, I held it together until I stood on top; more surprised than anything and, of course, delighted.

As happens when you climb a block you first saw a long time ago, it's nice to look back on the transformations that have happened since first sight.

As a wise old man once said to me, "Small hills lead to big mountains."

HIGHBALLING

Highballing is the term used for problems that are high enough for falling to cause injury or worse, even in the best case scenario for the landing. While there is no truly objective scale for calling a problem a highball, a good rule of thumb for height is somewhere between 15 and 20 feet, a height at which even a well-managed fall can have pretty serious consequences. With the use of big crashpads, a good deal of the risk can be managed, but at this height, ankles, knees, and backs are vulnerable to the huge impact forces created. Tall problems make different demands on the climber than shorter, steeper problems.

First, highballs have more moves and take longer to climb than the average five-move problem. The climber has to be careful to develop the endurance needed to stay in control near the top, where success is

A scary first ascent for Kevin Jorgeson on The Duel *(V10), Hueco Tanks* (Photo by Andy Mann)

Abbey Smith up high in Hueco Tanks
(Photo by Caroline Treadway)

essential. Nothing erodes confidence faster than tense and unbalanced footwork and shaky legs. You may need to climb for five or more minutes, so developing good resting and pacing skills is vital. Also important is smooth technique, especially for moves such as mantels or rockovers. If you have worked the moves on toprope (a process usually known as *headpointing*), make sure that you have a fully doable sequence that you can execute flawlessly. Even with the best spotters and a pile of pads, very bad things can come of big falls. Always go in with both eyes open.

To highball, a cool head is paramount. The ability to keep focused and confident in the face of potentially serious terrain is essential for anyone seeking to explore this kind of terrain. It becomes even more important if you decide to climb such a problem from the ground up. The highball boulderer treads a narrow path between security and disaster, especially if the crux is high on the problem. Therefore a very clear and honest assessment of your abilities and capability to handle stressful situations is mandatory to avoid a trip to the hospital. Never just "go for it," however tempting it seems. The best climbers have worked out to an extraordinary degree their chances of success on a problem and while total security is not a realistic option, success on such problems is more the product of rational calculation than sudden inspiration.

One tactic commonly used with highballing is carpeting the landing with many, many pads. While some problems might require only two or maybe three pads, some of the pad collections at the base of problems such as *Evilution* amount to twenty or more. Popular semi-highballs such as the *Mandala* are also well upholstered on any given day. *Remember that pads only reduce risk, they do not eliminate it.* The impact of a 20-foot fall is always substantial so be forewarned and aware.

One tactic used increasingly, as highballs begin to look more like free soloing, is headpointing. In headpointing, the climber works on the problem on toprope until he feels confident that a fall will not happen. The actual ascent is done without the rope, though usually with multiple pads in place. Headpointing tactics have met with some criticism, but remember that as long as you don't permanently alter the rock, your style of ascent is your own business. Often, the ground-up ascent of a tall problem that was first headpointed gets recognized by the community as well.

Just as with massive pad use, the headpoint tactic does not guarantee safety or security. Do not underestimate the mental challenge of embarking on a hard climb without the safety of a toprope. As mentioned above, specialists in the game of highballing calculate very carefully the margin between likely success and failure. They do not blindly enter into this realm of high-risk climbing but choose instead to study all the factors involved before making a decision. For them, attempting these problems implies not bravado and spontaneous inspiration, but a conscious choice. That is how they live to climb another day.

GETTING BACK DOWN

While getting up a problem is the goal of bouldering, the need to get back down safely should not be ignored. There are many boulders, for example, at the Buttermilks in California, where the easiest way up and down could be the problem you just did. You might have a tall, scary downclimb from a short, steep problem on the other side of the same boulder. Another scenario might have you doing a fairly long jump to another boulder or down to the ground. Topping out on a snowy boulder without having cleared a descent path could prove hazardous.

Anticipate these situations by studying the terrain closely before you head up, and have a contingency plan. Most guidebooks note descent routes if directions seem necessary so study the topo in advance. If you know that the descent is hazardous, have your spotter move the mats accordingly so that you have some margin of safety if possible. Work on your downclimbing skills, especially up high, to help find the safest way back down. It may even be worth climbing to the top to confirm the descent route as well as to scope out the top of the boulder for hidden holds or to clean off dirty ones.

The problem is not over until you are safely back on terra firma. Some serious injuries have occurred because of a lack of attention to descents. In many instances, especially with problems that have tall and chossy finishes, boulderers will drop off the problem at a big hold or other obvious

THE ART OF WILDERNESS BOULDERING

Jamie Emerson has hiked many, many miles in search of new boulders in the high mountains of Colorado and elsewhere including Alaska. His blog, B3bouldering.com is an insightful source for thoughts on the sport.

I have been bouldering for thirteen years. I am interested in many facets of climbing and I love adventure. I love the complexity of trying to fit my body around a piece of rock. There are so many different moves and shapes involved that I don't think it ever gets old. When I visit natural environments, I see how each one has its own characteristics, including its own plant and animal life.

One of the most attractive things about Colorado is that there are a lot of access points for people who want to get to the mountains quickly. This isn't always the case. In places like Montana and Wyoming, for example, it's a long hike to the boulders. Here, access points are really easy, so you can quickly get up into the mountains. There are so many boulders in the mountains—the talus fields are just ridiculous. I think it's the future; it's where bouldering is going. There are always fresh collections of boulders that offer new problems.

The rock in Rocky Mountain National Park is granite and gneiss, dramatically shaped by ancient glaciers and some of the severest weather on the planet. The environment is alpine, mostly above treeline and exposed to weather. Bouldering here feels a little more dangerous and a little more adventurous. You feel the altitude. You have to deal with thunder, lightning, and navigating huge blocks of talus. I like the challenges that weather, steep terrain, and complex environment present. They add an element of adventure that was missing before in the sport. Until now bouldering was always marginalized by traditional climbers because you were climbing on such small objectives. Alpine bouldering has to be taken much more seriously than a simple roadside session near town.

The mountains are such complex terrain to explore. I feel like there is an almost infinite variety of territory to investigate, a gigantic playground. But you have to get out there and look and not get discouraged. Go for a long hike and don't get focused on finding the next Chaos canyon or Mount Evans. You never know. You might find an entire talus field; other times it might be a boulder hiding in the woods. The reward of simply being in the mountains is always there, no matter what.

Jamie Emerson

stopping place. Confirm what the consensus is before you claim to have done the problem.

TRAVERSES

One practice in bouldering that is rarely encountered in roped climbing is traversing. Traversing refers to going across a feature rather than up it. Some can be a few moves long, while others can be hundreds of feet across. They require a different mindset compared to straight-up problems because of their length and the techniques required. Climbers used to problems of five to ten moves may find a route of thirty moderate moves with poor or no rests very challenging.

Traverses are a great way to build endurance for longer problems or train for routes, but the sideways motions they involve do not necessarily translate well into those other forms of climbing. They can also be a lot of fun and a good way to climb without needing a rope or partner. Despite the generally safe nature of this kind of problem, here are a couple of things to watch out for. One is the issue of pads and protecting cruxes. There may be a hard part with a bad landing at the beginning and at the end.

Colette McInerney bouldering at Hueco Tanks (Photo by Caroline Treadway)

You may want to have two, three, or more crashpads placed at strategic points along the bottom of the problem. Having a spotter to move the pads and generally keep you covered is always helpful. This person can also be handy in clearing the way for you (alerting other climbers, politely!) on a popular wall.

Be careful to avoid moves that stress the shoulders, especially wide spans and gastons that overload the rotator cuff in a bad way. Traverses can be particularly aggravating in this respect and overspecializing in them can leave a boulderer vulnerable to this kind of injury.

There is no substitute for the power and strength gained from working straight-up problems. The endurance derived from going across a wall is not the same as that derived from going straight up. So if you use climbing wall traverses for training, include sections that move up and down, and even back and forth, adding in diagonal moves and so on to more accurately mimic the conditions of typical outdoor routes or problems.

RESTING

Boulder problems in their purest form do not allow rests for most climbers attempting them, requiring constantly high levels of effort from beginning to end. Nevertheless, recognize that resting is not always a matter of finding a really good hold and recovering completely. Even on a problem at your physical limit, finding ways to limit your exertion or relax even a tiny bit can ease your passage on the moves to come.

The first principle of resting is limiting the load on your hands and arms. This can mean finding a good dropknee or stem that allows more weight on the feet. It might mean an effective heel hook or, even better, a solid kneebar that allows a hand or even two to be removed. Whatever combination of core strength and foot placement you can make work, even for a brief shake, is good enough. Find handholds that allow you to hang straight-armed from bone and tendon. A hand jam or solid finger jam could be very useful this way.

The second key to successful resting is learning how to relax even in the midst of great effort. It is easy to get caught up in the need for strength and power and continue to apply it when it's no longer necessary. Let gravity set you better in place, and your body's natural structure find the best positions. Loosen your posture and your facial expression. Relax. Smile. Breathe. Stop wasting mental energy and your physical energy will rebound.

If the rest is good enough, let go with one hand and shake the other, allowing blood to circulate and muscles to recharge. Some training experts advise raising your arms up to refresh blood and drain out waste matter. Typical boulder problems do not allow that kind of opportunity, but if you get a good jug, make the most of it, taking time to get ready for the next section.

However, don't take too much time and weaken the sense of momentum that can be helpful in pushing through. Balancing movement with resting, and relaxation with powering through is at the heart of mastering bouldering.

BREATHING

In many spiritual traditions, the role of breathing to focus the mind and induce mental clarity is extensively discussed. The same holds true in the realm of climbing. Breathing is more than a simple physiological necessity; it can alter your response to stress, enhance your perceptions of the world, and increase your power. The important principle to remember is awareness. If you are aware of how you breathe, you can modify it to suit the circumstances and better your chances of success. Succumb to instinct and you may be out of gas, and out of luck, that much quicker.

So how do we breathe better? Begin by focusing on breathing before the climbing even starts. Deep belly breaths draw in oxygen and relax the core muscles. A regular rhythm of breathing steadies your psychological state and allows you to focus on the task at hand, shutting out distraction and centering your mind.

On the problem, keeping your breathing deep and regular helps stave off muscle fatigue in two ways. First you are delivering much-needed oxygen to your circulatory system. Second you are reducing the load on your muscles by maintaining a more relaxed emotional state, one that draws less energy from your body by demanding less from your muscles. When you feel

relaxed, you climb relaxed, allowing your technique to be at its best and, again, using less energy.

Breathing can also aid in the focused application of power. A deep intake of breath and well-timed exhale helps you complete a hard move. If you inhale pulling into the move and exhale pushing out of it, you may find you have quite a bit more momentum and accuracy than if you mistimed or held your breath. The worst thing to do while climbing is to tense up and hold your breath. Among other problems, this behavior heightens your stress level, making you less attentive to technique. It causes your abdominal core to tighten, lessening your ability to move easily and transfer weight to your legs. And within seconds, much-needed oxygen will be in short supply, limiting your strength and raising your anxiety level higher.

So remember to breathe before, during, and after the problem. Maintaining deep and regular breathing could prove to be the key for a seemingly impossible move.

FALLING

A book on bouldering would be incomplete without a good discussion on how to fall, for one simple reason: you are going to fall, and, in fact, you will be falling a lot. Since this aspect of bouldering carries a high risk of injury, it is wise to get a sense of how to best do it.

There are two basic kinds of falls, planned and unplanned, and each type has different

Carlo Traverso comes off Loaded with Power *(V10), Hueco Tanks.* (Photo by Andy Mann)

rules. In a planned fall, the boulderer and spotter are in full agreement on the likely scenario and how to handle it. This could include a jump from a problem or a fall from a known crux section. These kinds of falls are the easiest to handle because the unknowns are kept to a minimum and the climber can focus on the best outcome in advance.

The unplanned fall is more dangerous and problematic, with risks for both spotter and boulderer—avoid it if you can. These are falls from "easy" sections, falls due to broken holds, or falls owing to sudden failure of friction or other factors. They are dangerous since they can result in awkward landings on unexpected terrain in positions that expose the body to objective dangers like sharp rocks. The degree to which the climber can anticipate possible falls and outcomes is the degree to which the problem becomes safer.

In the days before crashpads, climbers were much more careful about falling and some even developed catlike techniques like turning to land feet first to reduce the impact of bad landings. Certainly, without crashpads, the taller, harder problems were much more committing then, which worked to limit the number of bad falls. The use of crashpads may lull today's boulderers into a false sense of security about falling. This is perhaps why on too many visits to local gyms, I see climbers, especially beginners, emerging with ice-packs strapped onto an injury sustained in a fall. Falls should never be taken lightly.

BASIC PRINCIPLES OF FALLING

The first principle of falling is protecting the important parts of the body, and the second is safe absorption of energy by finding ways to deflect the impact and disperse the force of the fall. All other aspects pale in comparison. In particular, you must always watch that your head and spine don't sustain direct impacts from the ground or other surfaces. Other injuries heal relatively easily, but brain and nerve damage are much too serious to leave to chance. Outdoors, assess the landing zone carefully for any objects such as small boulders and tree stumps that present uneven or pointed surfaces. In the gym, falling on water bottles and chalkbags could turn an ankle or worse.

Falling is simple physics: Force equals mass multiplied by acceleration. A falling body can be moving quite quickly after only a few feet of vertical distance. Dissipating this force safely requires gradually slowing the speed of the climber with guidance from someone spotting and standing close by. Landing on a cushioned surface or fleshy part of the body and rolling upon impact all help dissipate the force of the fall.

One way to learn to fall better is to take a bunch of falls from a low height in a relatively safe location, such as a climbing gym with ample, thick mats. Remember that the second principle of falling is safe energy absorption, directing and dissipating the forces generated by your fall into substances and directions best able to handle it. The fall will end; the question is how. While feet, ankles, and knees are flexible, responsive, and strong, using them to handle falls alone is like using a manual transmission instead of the more efficient brakes to stop a car. Much better is to land on your side or rear end after an initial deflection of force and then to roll away or just collapse into the pads.

The biggest mistake you can make is to try to stick the landing like a gymnast. Nobody out there is watching and deducting points for a landing that isn't perfect. Your body will deduct months and years from your climbing career for badly managed landings. Do not attempt the sumo style landing where you plant your feet solidly and your knees absorb the impact as your chest comes down. You are at risk of blowing out your knees and ankles, especially if the landing is at all uneven. You could even bite off the tip of your tongue if your knees and chin were to meet. Even at relatively low heights, such a style of landing is dangerous.

Instead, plan on hitting the mats just barely with your feet as flat as possible, folding your knees immediately and then dropping onto your side, as relaxed as possible, touching down first with your hips and then your shoulders, and then, if you have room, pushing off a bit with your feet and rolling away. For landing safely on falls starting 8 feet or more off the ground, this is the safest way to fall. By following this series of steps you dissipate the force of the fall into as much mass over as long a time as possible.

When falling, do not lead with your hands, elbows, or shoulders. Falls of this nature often result in hazardous sprains or breaks to shoulders, elbows, and wrists, injuries that take a long time to heal and prevent constructive training while recuperating. You can get at least some strength training in while healing a broken leg or ankle that is impossible while healing from a broken wrist. Let the bigger, fleshier parts of your body take the hit, not delicate soft-tissue areas like those around ligaments or tendons in crucial joints.

Watch young children as they run and play and tumble. Being young and flexible, they tend simply to collapse in a heap and then get up laughing. I sometimes wonder if adult climbers are afraid of appearing undignified if they land by collapsing and rolling. I would rather be thought to look foolish than to later need hip replacement surgery or face a lengthy healing process with uncertain results.

This kind of full-body falling technique requires careful attention to the landing zone. Whether in a gym or outside, a dangerous place is the edge or corner of a crashpad or mat. This is because a foot landing on a corner or edge lands unevenly, with the toe or one side of the foot staying high while the rest of the foot goes lower. Nothing can roll an ankle faster. This is why I never recommend breaking a substantial fall with the lower body alone. Get the force off those vulnerable areas as quickly as possible by collapsing and rolling. And always make your landing zones as flat and broad as possible.

The spotter's role in falls is not to catch the falling climber but to stabilize her, slow down the fall, and direct her movement to a safe landing on a good surface. If you watch a good gymnastics coach, you realize that the most important tasks are to guide the gymnast through the routine and assist a safe landing. In bouldering, the spotter is there to provide backup and make sure that a fall ends safely.

Neither climber nor spotter can anticipate unplanned or out-of-control falls. The worst are falls that deposit the climber in a dangerous place or position. The former can be avoided by liberally covering the landing area with a stable mass of pads, leaving no possibility uncovered. Especially outside, such landing zones can be uneven. It may be advisable for the climber to take a few test falls to see how things line up in the best-case scenario to avoid unsafe landings. Harder to anticipate are falls that set the climber up poorly, leading with the head, shoulders, or arms. Here it is helpful for the climber to have quick reflexes and a relaxed approach to landing. Do not fight what happens, but go limp or roll into a ball so that however you hit, you are dissipating the force as evenly and safely as possible. Fighting the impact of a fall only pits vulnerable joints and limbs against overwhelming forces. A relaxed and alert fall has a much better chance of ending well than a fearful and tense one. And the boulderer who feels safer falling will feel safer climbing and be much more likely not to fall. Paradoxical perhaps, but true.

One of the best discussions of falling and spotting that I have seen is in Marc Bourdon's *Squamish Bouldering*. Here the author points out the crucial difference between falling in a closed or open position, a term borrowed from gymnastics. Closed joints are those that have no wiggle room: Imagine bending back a straight finger, knee, or elbow. Closed joints take the impact directly and can be severely injured as a result. So, for example, falling with straightened arms and bent-back wrists is an invitation to broken bones. Open joints resist impact better, and spreading out the impact of the fall is the best bet to avoid injury.

PRE-JUMPING

Sometimes when I have been intimidated by a high problem or uncertain landing, I will deliberately jump from the crux of the problem or near it to simulate a fall. This is only safe if the landing is well prepared and I am confident that I will be okay. I have found this to be similar to taking long safe falls while sport climbing. It clears up misconceptions and allows an optimistic and confident attitude while climbing. It also give some sense of the likely trajectory of a fall, allowing better anticipation of a landing.

Some suggest throwing something up against the boulder in the vicinity of the crux to guess where a likely fall will land. This is helpful but only if the likely fall trajectory is straight down. Many bouldering falls can be affected by swinging positions or violent outward movements caused by breaking holds. Eyeballing the situation and carpeting the area well with pads is probably more useful.

SPOTTING

With the advent of crashpads, the game of bouldering changed drastically in the mid-1990s. For many problems, spotting became a non-issue. The use of crashpads took the sting out of many previously committing problems. However, risk is still a big part of bouldering, and spotting is an essential part of managing it. Any number of twisted, sprained, or broken ankles testify to this basic truth: Every fall in bouldering is a groundfall. A good spot by a capable partner can provide the margin of confidence needed to succeed on the problem and maybe never even test the spot.

To make the spot successful, a few basic rules need to be followed and they can by summed up in SPOT: S = Stance, P = Preparation, O = Observation, and T = Tactics.

Stance: Generally the spotter stands close under the climber, with legs apart, knees bent, and hands positioned just above the climber's center of gravity. Proximity prevents acceleration of the climber, which helps limit impact forces. The footing should be secure and reliable, and nothing should be allowed to interfere with the movement of the spotter.

Preparation: The landing area has been cleared of extraneous gear, loose rocks, and branches, and the pads have been arranged for maximal use and effectiveness.

Observation: The spotter is continually observing the climber and the terrain, aware of any changes in the situation that may affect the safety of the climber.

Tactics: Both spotter and climber have a plan in place to maximize the effectiveness of the tools and people at hand to ensure a successful ascent.

Here's a description of good spotting practice in action. *Tommy's Arête* (V7) in Rocky Mountain National Park is a steeply overhung problem that goes over a very uneven talus landing. Several pads are required to prepare the base to a reasonable level of security. To further complicate matters, a large boulder rests just behind the problem, offering a backslapping slide down to the pads from the last crux. In the photo on page 117, the climber is being spotted on this last section in perfect form. The spotter's hands are at rib level, ready to guide her into the pile of pads at the base. Just out of the frame, a pad has been hung on the steep slab behind the problem, offering some protection in the event of a fall. While Tara didn't get the problem in this session, she tried it with the confidence that a safe outcome would be likely, regardless of whether she topped out or not.

The good spotter assists only in the event of a fall. A firm grasp just above the hips with both hands that helps place the climber in a safe location and position is the only technique that is needed. The fingers should be close together and the thumbs kept out of the way so that they will not poke the climber or get bent backward. Grabbing any part of the body other than the waist is asking for trouble and not just out of modesty concerns. Virtually every other part presents serious risk of injury to the climber or the spotter; for example, the

A good, close spot on a problem with a tricky landing, Tommy's Arête (V7), in Rocky Mountain National Park

spotter gets poked in the eye by a climber, or the climber is tipped upside down by a spotter grabbing a leg.

The actual motion of spotting should be vigorous and confident with the only aim of setting the climber in a good place. Much as with roped climbing, it is really important that the spotter not let his guard down until the boulderer is clearly safe. Turning away for even a moment when a climber is in a vulnerable place can spell disaster. If you need to move a pad, make sure you and the climber are in agreement on when and where in the problem. Otherwise, find another pad or ask another person to move it.

ADVANCED SPOTTING TECHNIQUES

The usual scenario for bouldering is one climber spotted by one or two partners whose job it is to make sure he lands safely on the mats. Due to the irregular terrain below some problems, other techniques are used. One of them is deflecting or rebounding the falling climber. This might involve shoving the climber away from a hazard to a safer landing where more pads and spotters await. It might be helpful for the person deflecting to wield a pad like a shield to provide a soft initial impact.

Another technique might require someone grabbing the climber from behind and setting him down in a safer place. For example, on *The Potato Chip* in Rocky Mountain National Park, the climber faces a final crux with a 10-foot drop to the pads below. There is a ledge directly behind this move that you

Jackie Hueftle has a back-up spotter on Atari *(V6) at Happy Boulders, in Bishop, California.* (Photo courtesy Jackie Hueftle)

can retreat to. If you go for it and come up short, you could swing back out and plunge down. Having a strong partner who can grab you by the waist and place you on the ledge is a huge asset. Close communication and quick reflexes are especially valuable here. If it is done wrong both climber and spotter may end up falling together which is potentially very hazardous.

Some landings are sloping and lead to big drop-offs where both spotter and climber are in danger. In such situations the spotter can be tied into a climbing rope that is anchored solidly, allowing him to confidently snag a falling climber without worrying about falling into the abyss. It is always the role of the climber to assume all risks presented by a problem, and spotters and climber should be in total agreement about when the point of no more assistance is reached. Photos of spotters with hands outstretched below a climber who is 20 feet up do not reflect reality. When someone falls from very high up, the most you can do as a spotter is hope the pads are in the right place, help the climber land upright, and prevent the climber from rebounding someplace else. The impact forces generated by a high fall should be handled by the pads and the falling climber. If you are climbing a tall problem, talk these issues over with your spotters before heading up. Spotters have been injured, sometimes substantially, by being in the wrong place for breaking someone's fall.

Another advanced spotting technique is power-spotting. This is supporting the boulderer's weight a bit, by holding them at the bottom of the ribs, as they try a move, in order to get a sense for the direction and motion required to succeed. Some swear by this tactic, but I have experienced mixed results from it. Power-spotting can be helpful if it gives the climber the confidence to complete the move, as in a very steep wall with an uneven landing below. But it is important that you do not inadvertently power-spot on an actual ascent of the boulder problem. Even a minor contact with a spotter, the ground, or other *off-route* feature, a move known as *dabbing*, can invalidate an ascent.

Spotting is a serious business and should not be approached casually by either climber or spotter. It requires practice, attention to detail, and a commitment to the task at hand. An attentive spotter can save the climber a great deal of worry so he can focus on what matters most: the climbing. A poor spot, however, can land a climber in the hospital.

PAD PLACEMENT AND LANDING PREPARATION

Adoption of the crashpad truly revolutionized bouldering. But like any tool, crashpads can be misused to the detriment of both boulderers and the environment. The primary principle to remember is that pads absorb the shock of a landing and nothing else. Their powers of absorption are limited. They cannot prevent twists, sprains, breaks, or worse. Most important of all, they cannot function when they are absent altogether or in the wrong place.

The ideal landing zone for a problem is a flat, semicircle extending out about as far as the problem is tall. This ideal landing lacks tree roots, boulders, gaps between boulders, or other natural obstacles. There are no

Daniel Woods working a problem in Hueco Tanks (Photo by Andy Mann)

drop-offs or other hazards present. While such ideal landings are rare, crashpads can go a long way to making them better.

Crashpads iron out any irregularities that could snare an ankle or worse. They can span cracks or other gaps or can help fill them. They can also be terraced to help level out steep landing areas. Draped over boulders, pads buffer sharp edges and angles that present a threat to the climber.

Pads can be secured and linked together on steep slabs to provide protection as well. Many boulder problems are steep overhangs above low-angled slabs. Here, using webbing, carabiners, and even skyhooks (metal hooks used in aid climbing), pads are anchored in place to another boulder,

spike, flake, or tree. Be careful not to anchor to something that could injure you if it moves. Another good idea might be to add rubber patches or use "stealth paint" (rubber particles suspended in cement) to the bottom of the pad to add sticky friction. I expect more and more pad companies will make this a standard feature.

Pads should always be placed with the environment in mind. Use as few pads as needed for the problem. Crushing small plants or trees with pads denudes the area and promotes erosion. Spreading pads over a broad area can kill vegetation, destroy cryptobioic soil, and create ugly scars that take a long time to heal. When carrying pads be careful not to force a more direct, damaging route through small trees and bushes. Stay on established, wide trails whenever the option exists. And when tackling talus, remember that pads alter your balance and center of gravity and can trip you up.

Keep dogs and children out of the way when you are bouldering. Dogs in particular find bouldering pads attractive to lie down on, which can be an issue when you want to move a pad—or land on one! But more common is the habit of both small children and dogs to run unexpectedly under climbers. Serious injuries or worse

can result. No more valuable bouldering lesson can be taught to children than that they should never climb, walk, or run beneath a climber.

The number of pads a boulderer should own is a personal decision. I rarely go out with fewer than two if I anticipate falling, and will often travel with two full-size and one half-pad. You can easily bind them together with a long piece of webbing and a couple of metal rings in what is called a trucker's hitch. The half-pad covers sit-starts (boulder problems that start from a sitting position on the ground), and the full

Generous use of pads can protect a poor landing. (Photo by Jackie Hueftle)

pads can be distributed according to the needs of the problem. If you are traveling with a larger group, pads can be combined and shared.

Pads do begin to wear out after a lot of use. While a worn-out pad is not as dangerous as a worn-out rope, landing on one is not much fun. When you can begin to feel the underlying features on the ground, it is time to retire the pad. A number of pad makers offer foam recycling, which is a great way to lessen the environmental effects of pad disposal. I move mine to a pile under my home wall where they can still find use.

In recent years, as boulderers have begun to hike longer and longer distances to try problems, some have reduced the onerous task of hauling pads by leaving pads at the boulders instead of bringing them back at the end of the day. In Colorado, for example, fierce debates have emerged as to the appropriateness of pad stashing. A number of well-known climbers have stored pads at areas such as Rocky Mountain National Park or Mount Evans. It certainly makes boulder problems at altitude much easier to climb.

For the most part, as long as the pads are kept out of view, are well-maintained, and removed at the end of the season, the practice is relatively environmentally neutral. They can, however, be considered littering. Most land managers take a dim view of gear stashes of any kind, and the sight of boulderers heading off to a day of hard bouldering with nothing but a light daypack could send the wrong signal.

It's unclear how this debate will be settled, but, at a minimum, find out the local ethic before attempting to stash pads, and do not be too surprised if they are not there when you return.

LANDING PREPARATION

Before deploying pads, it is a good idea to survey the landing and clean it up if needed. A low-impact way to do this is to carefully remove sticks, small boulders, or other objects to one side, and when you are done bouldering, either put them back into place or scatter them in a natural fashion out of range of the landing. Larger obstacles should be dealt with by effective pad placement whenever possible. Never remove trees, bushes, or large plants without the permission of land managers or property owners.

When putting down your gear, it is a really good idea to keep it confined to a small hardened area such as the top of a boulder. Carrying a small bag or sack for organizing it makes it easier to consolidate gear instead of strewing it about the base, creating a visual eyesore, and adding to the impact of your visit.

With the advent of talus field bouldering, where the landings are often very rough, it has become popular to stage landing areas by moving around smaller blocks of stone to fill in gaps and flatten landings. This kind of stonemason's work may cause issues with land managers and other boulderers and has a visual impact that runs against the "leave no trace" ethic that should be at the heart of the outdoors experience. Avoid moving rocks.

More subtle forms of landscaping could include building up a streamside boulder's landing area with small boulders to allow a pad to be placed on top and stay relatively dry. The same could be done with sticks or stones to fill in a muddy landing temporarily. Such measures are relatively low-impact and easily dispersed after use. Once they become permanent fixtures, a line has been crossed, and again land managers or the public may take notice. Landscaping is a gray area with no obvious boundaries. Some have abused this lack of definition by wholesale alteration of landings in otherwise remote natural locations, but most have tried to respect the environment while keeping safety in mind.

CLIMBING TACTICS

Perhaps the most helpful skills to acquire in bouldering are the mental ones, habits of mind that save energy and skin and allow swifter understanding of the problem's difficulties.

SEQUENCING

One of these tactics is sequencing, or setting in correct order the hand and foot placements, body positions, and other movements that the problem requires. Sometimes this knowledge is readily discernable and obvious to remember, but often it is not, especially in the midst of substantial physical and mental stress. With levels of fatigue it is easy to forget a crucial foothold or weight shift, and a small mistake can make relatively easy moves next to impossible.

Sequencing in bouldering is aided by the ability to easily see and in many cases touch the holds and features on a problem.

Tyler Landman on Jade (V14), Rocky Mountain National Park (Photo by Caroline Treadway)

If you are serious about succeeding quickly on a boulder problem, ten minutes spent closely observing its holds and features could save you hours of frustrating work.

Begin by finding the starting handholds, as these often provide essential clues about how the problem is going to proceed. Many problems have sit-starts on low holds that are not immediately obvious. Next, locate the starting feet. They may not necessarily be beneath the hands but may be above or to the side, or even a heel hook on the same hold. Then figure out the first move's most likely path.

Check for everything: Will you need one or more *intermediate* holds to get to the next handhold? For example, a hidden pocket or sidepull may be essential to the problem. Having located the next hand, figure out the next foothold. Be open-minded here and consider that several foot placements may be required to settle in place for the next move. Then keep repeating the process until you have a good idea of what you think you need to do. Ask other boulderers present for *beta* (sequence and hold information). With chalk, carefully mark, or *tick*, holds you think may be difficult to find, taking care to make sure you understand your body position and line of sight relative to those marks. Remember to brush your marks away when you're done climbing.

Stand on stacked pads or adjacent boulders or trees to thoroughly scan and feel the holds and visualize body positions. Bring a good toothbrush for scrubbing out old chalk or any other debris, such as dirt or leaves.

Some boulderers bring long brushes for exactly this purpose. Go around to the top to note any crucial holds you may need to finish the problem. The fewer the surprises, the better.

Then step back and make sure you understand the problem in its totality and are not missing an obvious feature or hold that a close-up approach may obscure. Many climbers find it useful to mime the hand movements up the problem a number of times to understand it better and commit it to memory. Doing this work of remembering can save you a great deal of time on the problem itself while climbing it, allowing a greater chance of success in fewer tries.

What you are really trying to do here, if you can, is to flash the problem. This means to succeed on your first try after learning everything you can about the problem. The more mental work you have completed up-front, the more likely that first attempt will succeed. And if it doesn't go first try, maybe it will go in that first session or the next. Remember that careful thought and planning can radically leverage physical strength.

FRICTION

Friction is the key to all forms of climbing and especially bouldering. Many problems seem to depend on ephemeral states of weather, season, time of day, and finger skin for success. In addition to power, every serious boulderer longs for good friction to aid in success. Not so many climbers understand how friction works.

A well-placed heel hook (Photo by Andrew Burr)

rubber is reconciling two opposite factors, the softness needed to allow the crystals to deform the rubber and the hardness needed to keep the rubber from deforming too much or disintegrating and letting go. Temperature affects stickiness: The best conditions for modern sticky rubber are cool temperatures, between freezing and about 50 degrees F. This is good news since those are often the best conditions for finger skin as well.

It is always advisable to keep your shoe rubber absolutely immaculate before starting a boulder problem. This allows the rubber to work at its highest level and helps keep the polishing of the footholds to a minimum. You can spit-clean shoe soles by spitting on the heel of your hand and rubbing the rubber until it is pure black and squeaks. A piece of sandpaper is helpful to lightly sand away older, oxidized rubber. At home, storing your shoes in a relatively cool dark place will ensure the rubber degrades more slowly.

Before climbing, make sure the footholds are also clean. Some people insist on chalking footholds but the chalk doesn't improve shoe friction; in fact, it harms it.

While climbing, place your feet as carefully as possible, and once committed to a move, don't try to adjust them—your foot could slip. Slippers work by using the muscles of the feet to keep them on the holds so stronger feet equal better friction. Careful and deliberate footwork, focusing on loading the hold as fully and accurately as possible, gets the best friction results out of your rubber.

Let's look at the three points of friction and how to make the most of them.

Shoe friction. Shoe rubber sticks to rock by allowing crystals to dig into the surface, grabbing the shoe and stopping it from moving. The secret to effective shoe

Clothing friction. There are definitely times when you will want to use your legs to grip a feature such as a large sloper or outside corner. The best friction here is cotton canvas or denim. Most synthetics are too thin or slippery for this application though some boulderers will simply tape a kneepad to the leg just above the knee on the thigh. The best, all-purpose option is a pair of sturdy trousers made of natural material. This also grabs onto pad material better making for more secure landings, especially on sloping terrain.

Hand friction. No other topic has boulderers so frustrated so much of the time. Just as with rubber, you want to have skin that is soft enough to deform yet hard enough to bear weight without tearing or slipping. The catch is that you also need sensitivity as well. These mutually antagonistic demands, combined with the variables of weather, humidity, and rock type, make perfect friction as elusive as the Holy Grail. But you can maximize your chances by keeping the following ideas in mind.

Make sure your hands are clean and grease free. Never apply sunscreen with fingertips; use the back of your hand instead. Smooth out small tears or skin flaps with a clipper and emery board. Apply tape to finger splits or cuts, or better yet, wait to climb another day.

Next, apply chalk. This should be done deliberately, coating your fingers lightly and evenly and working the chalk into the skin. Once you have thoroughly dried your skin with chalk, remove the excess by blowing it off or flicking it back into the chalkbag. Spraying chalk everywhere is inconsiderate and annoying, especially in the gym. Once your hands are fairly white and dry, close up the chalkbag and start to climb.

Some climbers like to apply chalk to holds before climbing and this may have some benefit, provided it is minimal and doesn't interfere with the friction of the natural rock. Any excess should be brushed off immediately afterward. Artificial holds can especially benefit from this treatment. The various plastics and resin used in their manufacture can leave a slippery feel best removed with a light layer of chalk and a bit of brushing. Older holds in a home gym should be washed from time to time if necessary. Some climbers use rubbing alcohol to clean holds.

Good skin friction is the key to fun bouldering; chalk up for best results. (Photo by Jackie Hueftle)

Many boulderers don't climb with a chalkbag. You can rarely let go on a hard problem to chalk up, you don't need the extra weight, and falling with a chalkbag can create a huge mess, spilling chalk and making big dust clouds. *Chalk up* well before you leave the ground. On a longer problem such as a roof or a traverse, some boulderers have someone ready with a chalkbag at a convenient spot so they can chalk up before heading up higher off the ground or doing a particularly hard section. In some situations, such as highballing, you will want to carry a chalkbag.

There is such a thing as too dry an atmosphere. If your hands are fairly dry by nature, friction in really dry conditions can be a problem. This is most common when toughened cool skin meets hard dry rock, a more typical situation in winter. Boulderers describe their fingertips as being "glassy" and not gripping well. There are a couple of remedies for this. First make sure that your hands are warmed up and kept warm as much as possible. Second, use sandpaper or an emery board on slightly dampened fingertips to soften up calluses before chalking up. A little fine abrasion will open up the texture on your tips and soften them for better grip.

Calluses in general are the skin's protective response to stress from friction and impact. They are important to develop to protect your hands when bouldering on rough rock types on small holds. Yet calluses can be a double-edged sword if they become too hard and unresponsive to rock texture or are prone to cracking and ripping.

Boulderers are notorious for constantly sanding their fingertips for this reason. Keeping fresh, stickier skin at the surface and minimizing small flaps, creases, and tears makes for a longer and more productive session.

Some chalks come with drying agents that are intended to enhance friction. These can be very effective, in fact too effective, creating the glassy conditions I described above and also drying out and cracking skin. Since chalk is affordable, experiment with different brands and preparations to see what works best for you.

Use chalk the way it's meant to be used, in efficient doses. It is not sticky by itself and does not work better in large quantities. For the best friction, keep a bare minimum on your fingers and make sure you have removed as much chalk as possible from the holds to begin with. Keep

Brushing keeps the holds clean.
(Photo by Andy Mann)

your finger skin in good shape and make sure your hands are well moisturized after climbing. Some obsessed climbers will not put their hands in water, thinking this will keep the skin in better condition. Immersion in water, especially hot water, removes moisturizing oils from the skin, but the problem is easily remedied with any simple hand moisturizer. So feel free to shower or do dishes, or at least don't use your project as an excuse not to.

CLIMBING YEAR-ROUND

Each season has its own challenges but extremes of heat in summer and cold in winter present particular problems.

Generally, cool conditions, around 50 to 60 degrees F are best for bouldering so plan accordingly.

In most temperate climates, spring and fall are great times to boulder and many climbers are especially motivated for these times of the year. Even so, if you plan on making the most of your climbing time, you will want to persist even in relatively poor or unlikely conditions. To get the most out of less than ideal conditions, it really helps to plan ahead in terms of location, timing, and equipment.

The hardest conditions to climb something hard might well be in summer. Warm temperatures soften skin and reduce rubber friction, and warm air holds more moisture. The best strategy is to climb very early in

Austin Manning topping out an arête on a fall day (Photo by Andy Mann)

Daniel Woods on The Game *(V15), Boulder Canyon* (Photo by Andy Mann)

the morning or very late in the day, even at night. A good, lightweight headlamp can help with this. Make sure you choose problems that do not get direct sun, are preferably north- or west-facing, and do not have slopers or other friction-dependent moves. Drink plenty of water, bring lots of chalk, and dress lightly. The most popular strategy in Colorado, for example, is to visit alpine bouldering areas where the elevation is above 10,000 feet (3000 meters).

Winter conditions can be just as challenging since fingers go numb quickly and energy and motivation drains away. For the most part, temperatures much below 40 degrees F are going to be too severe for a productive bouldering session. The first principle is conservation of heat at all costs. This means warming up well, even before you reach the boulders. Overdress in multiple layers topped by a puffy down parka and do ten to fifteen minutes of aerobic exercise. If the approach is steep and long, all the better. Make sure you have a very warm hat and mittens (better than gloves since they allow hand warmers to be stashed in them) and keep them on all the time you are not actually climbing. Being overheated gets more blood to the extremities.

Bring a thermos of a warm, sugary drink such as cocoa or sweetened tea as well as snacks that can be eaten when cold. Many brands of energy bars harden to iron when cooled below 40 degrees F. Drink and eat often between attempts. Keep your shoes warm when they are not on your feet. And even with all this, plan on the session being short and to the point.

Do not build fires or bring portable heaters. If it's that cold, head instead to the warmth and sociability of the local gym. Most public land managers and private landowners take a dim view of fires being started on their land, even in winter. The heat that matters most in winter bouldering is the heat that comes from within.

GRADES AND HOW TO USE THEM

John Sherman has expressed regret at inventing the V scale (he claimed it fostered competition and commercialism in bouldering); yet some kind of relatively objective open-ended rating system for bouldering was inevitable. Difficulty ratings emerged in rock climbing early on and a specialized one for bouldering was a logical step.

There had been steps in that direction with the creation of grades below B1, such B5.9, B5.10, and so on, sometimes with plus or minus added. B1 was supposed to mark where real bouldering came in, above previously achieved roped grades. However that changed and B1 marked a spot around 5.11 + /5.12 while B.5.8, etc. was used for lower grades. The issue with this system was that it confused bouldering difficulty with roped difficulty and tended to compress the grade, by placing a wide range of actual difficulties in a single slot.

Enter the V grade. In Hueco Tanks, where there are literally thousands of recognized problems and variations, something was needed to make a common-sense assessment of difficulty, a scale that stood apart from the traditional scale for roped climbing. The V grade originally started at V0, terrain that might compare to roughly 5.9 in difficulty. In Hueco, a V0 might be a bit past vertical, with mostly very good holds and maybe one or two moves on smaller holds, terrain that is very common in that area. V1–V4 is more difficult, V4 being comparable to a crux on a 5.12 rock climb. Here the terrain might be quite overhung and sustained on decent holds, or vertical with small crimps.

Seriously difficult bouldering begins, in my view, at V5 or V6. Here even the experienced boulderer is going to have to work hard for success on the problem. Complex sequences, dynamic movement, very small holds, and sloping holds are all likely to be encountered from here on out. At V8 or V9, you are certainly climbing at an expert level, and V11 to V13 is about average for an elite-level boulderer. V14 and V15 are common only among a dedicated crew of full-time climbers, and V16, at the time of writing, is still hypothetical, since a number of problems have been proposed in this grade but none confirmed.

So how can we make sense of the rating system? To understand it better, you need to join the community of boulderers, spend time working on problems of all different grades and styles, and go to different areas. Beginning boulderers start in the VB range (problems easier than V0) to about V1 or V2. In older areas especially, there are often V1s and V2s that must be treated with respect since undergrading (ratings less than the actual difficulty of the problem) is common in this range. Here the problem might feel hard for the grade. In newer areas, where consensus is still being worked out, you may find higher rated problems that feel *soft* for the grade. Many expert boulderers, competent in the range of V11 and up, find themselves stopped cold by problems in the V6 to V8 range that don't suit their favored style of climbing or their body size.

Use grades as a rough guideline for helping you decide what you want to climb. Some problems fit some climbers much better than other. Conditions, seasonal factors, and missing beta can radically transform difficulty. Some climbers favor certain rock types or kinds of holds over others; for example, they might feel strong on slopers or crimps and weak on pinches.

A big problem emerges when boulderers decide to climb a problem for the grade. For example, wanting to have a V10 in your collection of ascents, you might choose a climb that appears to suit you, even though it isn't really very good: It lacks a good line, is really low to the ground, or includes *contrived* moves. You spend a lot of time on it and can't quite get it, and become frustrated as a result. Then you fail on some V8s and see your self-esteem plummet further. "I should be able to climb this problem" is a common indicator that this is happening. Soon motivation drops even

further as your vision of what you should be climbing conflicts with what you actually can climb.

When the grade drives the process, dissatisfaction and frustration result much faster than when the climb itself drives your bouldering choices. The climb that you really want to do for its own sake is the one that you actually stand the best chance of doing. The climb you do for external reasons, like reputation or grade, is the one that will sap your motivation the quickest. That is not to say that grades can't motivate you. If the climb is attractive and of a difficulty that you have never reached before, a grade, like any other milestone, can provide that little bit of incentive to make you work harder and build up the strength and skill you need to succeed.

The best way to use grades to build confidence is to have a solid pyramid of ascents below the next progression you want to make. If you want to climb a V7, a good start is to have completed at least three or four ascents of V6 problems of different styles and in different areas before you work on the 7. Having this background can help in dealing with the increased level of difficulty by letting you appraise the challenge of a higher standard more objectively. It also encourages you to try problems that are recognized as being solid at the grade, meaning your accomplishment can be better built on, as opposed to a lucky send of a soft V7 that suited your body type and climbing style. Trying a soft V7 with only a few V5s under your belt may work out all right if the problem suits you, but the next

BOULDERING AND BELIEF

Alex Johnson has climbed several V12 problems, often in very rapid times. She is one of the most successful competitors on the American and world circuits.

I started climbing at age seven on a portable wall at a county fair in Wisconsin, many hours away from any major climbing area. I got a day pass to a local gym (in a grain elevator!), won a competition in my age division, and things went on from there. What drew me to bouldering eventually was that its social aspect made it more fun. As a teenage girl I had to climb with young men which helped define my climbing style and my passion for climbing. I would like to see more women going out together as a group, sharing ideas and energy the way men do. Women are capable of trying hard and succeeding on hard problems.

My first hard boulder was *Sunspot* (V10/11). It was my second trip to Rocky Mountain National Park. I did the moves quickly and then just climbed it, first try. I was in shock. It turned me toward bouldering outside. I said to myself, "I can do this!" The next problem I did was *Clear Blue Skies* (V11/12). I spent time working each move and after an hour, topped out the boulder. Despite my success on these harder problems, I still get frustrated on much easier problems.

Bouldering outside is so important to me now, perhaps because I didn't have that experience growing up. I wish more girls and women would be adventurous that way. You don't have to go on a seven-mile hike searching for new boulder problems, but just get outside and climb. Having confidence in your climbing is huge. You don't have to look up to a guy for inspiration. If you believe in yourself and go for it, you will most likely stick the move and do the problem.

Alex Johnson

V7 you attempt may simply shut you down and erase the confidence you had in your ability. Better to build solid foundations of climbing skills and strength, working through the grades as you go, and accepting that some problems will feel easy, some will feel hard, and some may simply never go, even if you are solid at the grade.

The V grade is the standard American system, but there is also an international scale, based more or less on the system invented at Fontainebleau. This *Font* grade is similar to the French roped-climbing scale in that there is an Fb prefix, then a number followed by a letter, as in "Fb 8a," for example, and then a plus if needed. You may also see a F 8A, where the capital letter implies bouldering. Here is a sample of the progression: 6a, 6a+, 6b, 6b+, 6c, 6c+, 7a, 7a+, 7b, and so on. For a few comparisons to the V scale, 6c is roughly equivalent to V5, 7a+ to V7, 7c to V9, 8a to V11, and 8b to V13. V0 would be about 5c in the French scale. It is worth noting that many expert boulderers have gone to Fontainebleau and been unable to do 6a problems and then flashed 7c or harder on others.

A variant of the Font grade is given for traverses. Traverses are seen in Europe as different from straight-up problems, since they involve endurance more than power and are graded more like traditional routes. If you travel, it's a good idea to be familiar with the Font system as it is the international standard. Even in Germany, where for sport climbing most areas still use the obscure UIAA scale of Roman numerals, bouldering grades are given using the Font system.

It is common for indoor climbing walls to adopt an in-house system that is altogether different. For example, taped problems at the Spot, a popular gym in Boulder, Colorado, are graded with a spot scale where red dots with pluses or minuses are taped at the base of the problem. Other gyms may use a category such as "novice" or "elite" to grade their problems. These systems are useful for sorting out what problems might be worth trying, but as with V or Font grades, they are just labels and should not be taken too seriously.

As a rough guide to your ability, gym grades can give structure to a training program but should never be considered as absolute. It's better to develop your own sense of your ability and strength as you grow and develop as a climber and not be too quick to attach a label and a number to a problem.

Especially at the higher grades, boulderers will assign different grades to different methods, variations, sit-starts, and eliminates (off-route holds or features). If you want to claim an ascent and a grade, it is advisable to do some research. For some problems, the difference between a true *sit-start* and a sit-start off a stack of pads is huge. On others an obvious hold or feature may be off-route. On yet others, a variant finish is mandatory to claim the grade.

These kinds of minutiae are one of the aspects of bouldering that some find off-putting and others enjoy. The choice is yours. Pick the lines and moves that appeal to you regardless of the grade, and focus on enjoying the experience. When you learn this way, the lessons and skills you acquire will stick with you longer and reinforce your ability to cope with different types of rock and moves as well as to develop new techniques.

CLIMBING IN THE GYM

For most, a good session outside always seems more rewarding than a gym session. Yet there are aspects to the gym experience that are worthy in their own right. And for training for outdoor bouldering, especially if you are on a tight schedule, artificial walls are simply a necessity and a fact of life. Let's discuss how to make the most of your time indoors.

There are some issues with gym climbing. The gym is never a substitute for climbing outside. There are too many

With many holds in a small place, the gym is a great place to learn to boulder better.

differences for any climber to automatically assume that an ability to climb hard inside translates to similar results outside or vice versa. The ease of access (you are more likely to visit more often, leading to overuse injuries) and availability of hard terrain and moves makes injury much more likely. The social setting can distract and complicate things for even the most dedicated athlete.

The first important fact to remember about gym climbing is that manufactured climbing holds rarely get close to the shapes and sensations of natural holds on real rock. Hold companies offer curved radiuses, smooth textures, and thumb-friendly shapes. Route setters will often set problems that play to these characteristics, building in long dynamic moves between fairly large handholds. The differences in footholds are even more pronounced with the smallest jibs in the gym being three or four times as wide as typical holds outdoors.

The movements between features on natural rock are performed by humans, but they are not designed by humans. Larger holds require less precision in placement or attention to textures. A steady diet of gym climbing prepares you poorly for the often small, rough handholds, awkward technical moves, and practically invisible feet placements typical of outdoor bouldering.

A small *thumbcatch*, a shift in the hip or angle of a knee, a miniscule crystal for a foot: These minor features or tactics found readily, though unpredictably, outside are often absent in the gym setting. This is not to imply that gym climbing is devoid of subtlety, just that it is necessarily simpler than climbing outdoors.

Furthermore the usually steeply overhung nature of many walls favors dynamic movement on relatively incut hands and feet or large, somewhat sloping holds. Many well-known bouldering test pieces outdoors are on walls that are relatively low angle compared to the average climbing wall. The difficulty comes from the small size of the holds, their angle and position, and the texture of the rock. Thus a gym-trained climber may experience success on steep problems of a certain grade and be shut down by more technical problems of a lower grade. The smart boulderer works on all aspects of bouldering, including low-angle technical problems.

Finally the landings in a gym setting are generally so friendly and the walls so much higher that a false sense of confidence can emerge about your security climbing outside on a shorter problem. Remember that even a good-sized pile of mats offers little security compared to the flooring in a gym, and a conservative approach to falling outside, and indeed inside, is always best. Plan your landings and use a spotter. Develop the skills to fall safely, as described elsewhere in the book, by remembering to dissipate impact forces through good spotting, and collapsing and rolling when possible.

The gym is a very useful tool for training. The rich concentration of diverse holds and walls makes it possible to accomplish amounts of intense pure climbing impossible to replicate outside. However, the concentrated intensity of the experience opens up the possibility of injury through chronic overuse and even abuse of the body. Relentlessly steep angles and a heavy diet of dynamic moves deliver a beating to shoulders and elbows. Fingers get their fair share of abuse with repeated tries on hard problems. Good habits and warm-up routines (described in the next chapter on training and injury prevention) are important. After a few weeks of repeated heavy sessions, with no downtime or easy sessions (after all, you must be getting stronger right?), you may start feeling tight in your forearms, have low energy levels, and begin to see your performance slip as well. This is not because you are not working hard enough, it is because you are not resting well and diversifying your climbing regimen.

Finally, the social scene at the local wall presents its own problems. It is distracting; people chat rather than climb productively. Another social problem is going along with what your friends want to do. This can be a useful way to break out of your rut by trying moves or problems you might not normally undertake. But it can also undermine a session by sidetracking your plans to work on a specific problem or weakness.

Sometimes the social setting can be beneficial, sometimes not. Are you climbing with others to show off and for bragging rights or are you working hard on your own climbing and learning by watching them climb or spotting? Make sure you learn the difference.

WOMEN AND BOULDERING

It is heartening to see the degree to which women have enthusiastically taken up the sport of bouldering. As someone who began climbing when the sport was totally dominated by men, I can say that the fresh perspectives and attitudes that women bring to bouldering are welcome. Stereotypes and assumptions about bouldering being the province of men have begun to fade.

Although women are on average shorter than men and have less lean muscle mass as a percentage of total body mass than men, power and reach are only part of the story in a sport where success is driven by technique.

Like men, women who take up bouldering should initially focus on developing technique and strong fingers; the overall body strength will follow. Climber Jackie Hueftle, comments on her development as a

Abbey Smith reaches for a hold.
(Photo by Andrew Burr)

boulderer: "I think the most helpful thing to me in improving at bouldering was strength training. When I started climbing I had almost no muscle, and as a sport climber I learned to hang long and lean on my bones and bend my arms as little as possible. Bouldering, on the other hand, demands almost constant tension and constant arm-bending. I feel like the muscle I gained comes back more quickly and gives me a higher overall level of fitness for all kinds of climbing I participate in."

The tendency for women to have a greater proportion of body fat than men is not that much of a problem either. A sensible diet and general fitness is all that is required here. At the very highest grades, the temptation is to imagine that a pound or two less would make the difference. It is a lot easier and healthier, however, to lose that pound by using your feet better or working on your technique to lessen the load on your arms and fingers. Unfortunately, as in many sports, eating disorders are much more common among women climbers than their male counterparts, and in my view are a sad comment on misplaced priorities in the sport, i.e., valuing strength and weight over technique. As the father of a daughter, I know I would rather see healthy, powerful female athletes performing at their best than emaciated unhealthy ones.

Women inevitably have different relationships with their bodies than men do. I encourage boulderers of either sex to climb with women, as well as with men. I always learn from different climbers even if I can't climb as well as they can. The psychological lift that comes from seeing others achieve the seemingly impossible using differing techniques and body-mind approaches can be really useful in resolving your own strength issues.

The best path to follow as a climber, male or female, is your own path. This can include first ascents. Abbey Smith, prominent boulderer and writer, advocates for women to be more active this way: "Women should get out there exploring their own first ascents." Avoid stereotypes that confine and restrict you as a climber.

SUMMING UP

I have tried to emphasize throughout this book that mental effort conserves physical resources and promotes mastery of the skills required for safe and fun bouldering. Every boulderer should be aware of ways in which they can make the game more rewarding and effective. Here are some simple suggestions that can help you get the most from every session.

1. Plan for the season and time of day. Does it make sense to try that sloping compression problem in the heat of the full afternoon sun, or with hands frozen in winter?

2. Make sure you have everything you need: Good edging shoes? Plenty of chalk and tape? The right clothes for the climate?

3. Do your homework on boulder problems and areas. Don't waste time on the wrong approach or poor climbing. Use a guidebook or local beta online to sort through the chaff. Internet videos are a great source for information as well as motivation. Ask around before you spend an hour driving in circles or getting lost hiking.

4. Cultivate good partners. If your partners are apathetic or careless, a bad day could be in store. Don't risk ruining a long day with this kind of company. The gym is a good place to get a read on other boulderers.

5. Prepare the landing area. Elsewhere I describe the steps to take to ensure a safe landing. Make sure this is done on even the most innocuous boulder problems. Your ankles will thank you.

6. Stop when you are tired or out of sorts. Most injuries occur when climbers are tired and using poor judgment about their physical and mental capacity. Do everything you can to stay fed and hydrated and strong, but also know when to call it a day.

One piece of wisdom that highball master Jason Kehl offers is useful when things aren't starting off well: "He who can laugh falling off his warm-ups will send his project." Keep the long view in mind and rewards will come.

CHAPTER 5

Chad Greedy on The Kind Traverse (V11), Rocky Mountain National Park (Photo by Caroline Treadway)

Training and Injury Prevention

BASIC PRINCIPLES OF TRAINING

Becoming a better climber is a combination of many factors. While I think that climbing itself is usually the best way to get better, there is no doubt that training away from real rock is an important part of the serious climber's routine. In this chapter, I hope to show you some ways to get the best results from training. The stronger you are, both physically and mentally, the better time you are likely to have when bouldering.

CLIMBING PHYSIOLOGY

Understanding a few basic concepts about exercise physiology will help you become a better climber. First and foremost are the concepts of overload and supercompensation. To get stronger, you must work at a level your body is unaccustomed to. After a recovery period, your body rebuilds and adapts to the new level of stress you have put on it. Getting stronger as a climber means knowing when and how to raise the workload on your body.

Climbers rely on anaerobic energy, a byproduct of which is lactic acid. Training your body to adapt to the anaerobic conditions that occur at close-to-maximum short-term effort is an important goal of physical training for climbing. Aerobic, long-term effort is rarely important in comparison.

WARMING UP

Warming up is an important part of training as well as any climbing session. By putting in fifteen to twenty minutes of light exercise, such as easy climbing, running, or even a hike to the boulders, you prepare yourself for the work ahead by raising your heart-rate, warming your joints and musc les, and readying yourself mentally. I prefer to keep my warm-up routine flexible, allowing myself the option to shorten or extend it depending on how I am feeling. However, I find that overall, a session that starts with

Daniel Woods on Desperanza *(V15), Hueco Tanks* (Photo by Andy Mann)

a good warmup goes much better than one that starts hard right away.

SPORT SPECIFICITY

Every book on training for a sport emphasizes this fundamental truth: You cannot get better at something by working at something else. For bouldering, focus on improving skills specific to climbing. Even seemingly related activities such as pull-ups and working out on a campus board are only marginally useful in making you a better climber. Always focus on developing strengths and skills specific to climbing.

CREATIVE TRAINING

Dave Wahl, climbing coach, proposes that climbers focus on biomechanics, physiological adaptation, motor development, and climbing's psychosocial and mental aspects.

To advance and improve, you must think creatively and holistically both about your climbing and your preparation for climbing. The whole climber needs to assess and respond to training, not just bits and pieces at a time.

VOLUME AND INTENSITY

To build strength and ability in bouldering, steadily increase both the volume and the intensity of your climbing through your training regimen. In order to increase the load on your body, you must understand these two basic avenues and how they work together. Increasing the sheer amount of climbing you do is especially useful for the beginning climber. Here you simply increase the amount of time spent working at your current level. This approach is great for developing much better technique and getting the movement patterns in place to move to the next level. As long as you do not increase the intensity and you rest well, the likelihood of injury is low.

The volume strategy has its limits in achieving higher levels of difficulty. At some point, you will have to raise the intensity of your climbing sessions. If you have been quickly climbing twenty V0s to V2s in a session, try working on five or so problems from V3 to V5 for a while, focusing on exerting maximal effort in a brief time. As you achieve the next level, you can begin to emphasize volume once again. Training well is often a process of balancing the two strategies and finding the right mix, seeking always to avoid the plateau effect.

SUPERCOMPENSATION

Your body has the ability to bounce back from high levels of exertion, to adapt and recover, and to become stronger. While there is a genetic component limiting the extent to which you can develop and adapt physically, most climbers are far from finding those limits. Climbing, since it is so technique-dependent, is affected less by physiological issues than by technique, psychological factors, resources, and life circumstances.

You adapt to stresses in training by adding more muscle mass (hypertrophy) and by developing the ability of those muscles to work efficiently (recruitment). For most climbers, hypertrophy is of limited use but maximal recruitment is very important. Adding mass means you must carry more

weight on the rock, while better recruitment gets more out of what is already there.

As discussed below, you do not get stronger just from working your muscles. You get stronger from recovery periods in between, when your body puts things back together stronger than before. Failure to adequately rest can lead to general fatigue, illness, and injury.

POWER

If there is one thing every boulderer ultimately wants, it is more power, the ability to apply force quickly. Power helps in so many ways, whether you are pulling hard to generate force for a long-reach dyno, rapidly latching onto a bad hold, or pressing smoothly up into a mantel. Power can also be easily misapplied. Climbing is such a technique-oriented sport that almost regardless of the move or position, it pays to be very attentive to how power is used.

If you are misusing a foothold, for instance, you may be creating a situation that no amount of power can resolve. In fact by overpowering a poor placement, you run the risk of serious injury as you load unprepared tendons and muscles. An effective foot placement can decrease the weight your fingers bear by half or more. Even a very small edge on a very steep wall can support a substantial proportion of your body weight, especially when you bring your core muscles properly into play.

Remember that in most positions in climbing, you are typically dealing with loads on your arms and fingers well below body weight. Climbing is not gymnastics,

Phil Schaal on the Hueco problem, Alma Blanca *(V13)* (Photo by Andy Mann)

though a background in gymnastics training may help your bouldering ability immensely. Therefore, it is always helpful to use only as much force as the move requires. Top-notch climber Alexander Huber may have said, as he was getting ready to free the Salathé Wall on El Capitan, "It's okay, I have power to waste," but years of successful climbing gave him that confidence and overabundance of ability and power. Few of us can say that we have that much power to spare, yet much of the time we are all doing just that, wasting power. We waste it learning the moves, overcoming fear, dealing with frustration, and imitating our friends.

Being aware of what you are doing and feeling is the best way to overcome the temptation to burn up power. Sure, sometimes, to make a hard problem happen, you need to step on the gas; and in actual training, careful overload is the key to building strength. But in the course of actually doing a problem, most find they wind up using far less power than they thought necessary. "The problem felt easy," is a common refrain, the reason being that the climber thoroughly understood what the problem required. As philosopher and scientist Francis Bacon famously wrote, "Knowledge is power."

HOW TO TRAIN FOR POWER

In climbing it is easy to measure the maximum static load your body can withstand. What is the smallest hold you can hang onto? How much weight can you add and still hang on with both hands? How long can you hang on an edge with one hand? Even in the active mode of strength measurement, such baseline measurements are possible. For example, how much weight can you add and still do a single two-hand pull-up? Can you do a one-arm pull-up? What rungs can you reach on a campus board? And so on.

But power is more than that: It is the capacity to apply force quickly. For bouldering, power involves both movement and control, benchmarks that do not necessarily translate well into the complex art of moving through and between static loads. Climbing is never entirely static so merely hanging on an edge singlehanded is minimally applicable compared to being able to powerfully pull or push a long way off the same edge. Even relatively static (isometric) muscle applications such as gripping a hold involve dynamic shifts of position through elbows, wrists, and fingers as the body position changes relative to a hold. More dynamic exercises reflect controlled situations at odds with most climbing movements. Rarely is a climbing move similar to a pull-up, and even campusing—with its helpful emphasis on pulling and pushing through a move cycle—has little in common with the majority of situations encountered in bouldering.

FINGER STRENGTH AND FINGERBOARDS

So what does the climber who wants to improve her power do next? I think that the belief that you can never have fingers that are too strong is pretty well founded. Anything that builds finger strength is going to be helpful.

A simple session on a fingerboard is a good place to begin. A thorough warm-up on easy hangs or short problems lasting at least fifteen to twenty minutes is essential. Next, run through different grip positions, number of fingers, and types of holds, starting with the easiest and moving to the hardest. Hanging on with both hands is typical, and reducing the load by using a chair or counterbalanced weight can be useful. If you cannot load at least 75 percent of your body weight onto the holds for at least five seconds, you should probably focus on

A fingerboard is a great way to build finger strength.

climbing more on bigger holds to build up finger strength.

Climbers who can easily hold their body weight on two hands, on whatever size hold, should consider doing one-hand hangs and adding weight. Pull-ups are not necessarily helpful as part of a fingerboard workout. Any hold that you can stay on for more than fifteen seconds is probably too big. Minimal rests between hangs and sets of hangs makes sense, though you ultimately will want to wind up reasonably fresh at the end.

A fingerboard workout should not be about endurance and should last less than an hour in total. Wills Young, a powerful boulderer residing in Bishop, says, "Always leave something in the tank. Try to improve the weakest aspects of your climbing first for maximum gains." It's good advice.

When using a fingerboard, try to start and finish reasonably fresh. Hydrate well before and after to minimize tendon irritation, and limit use of such workouts to once a week or so. Oppositional stretches and exercises are essential for limiting the constant tension on tendon attachments that leads to tendonitis. Stay away from dynamically loading your fingers, especially in a closed, crimp position, and favor open-handed grips whenever possible.

UPPER ARM STRENGTH

Moving into the upper arms, you can develop strength in a number of ways, though to make gains in power your training time might be better spent climbing instead. Still, there are several ways to build upper arm strength, including weighted pull-ups or lat pull-downs on a weight machine. The idea is to overload the muscles of the upper arm and back while pulling in. Part of the challenge is deciding whether speed should be a factor in doing the exercise as rarely is a pulling motion on a hard problem done slowly. To avoid injury, I recommend steady and carefully applied force rather than rapid, jerking pulls. The total number of repetitions for this kind of exercise should be around three, max.

Note that in the fingers and arms, bigger muscles add mass and hence strength more rapidly than the connective tissues such as tendons. This imbalance of strength can quickly result in tendonitis, muscle pulls, and even stress fractures. There are no quick fixes to building lasting, safe strength gains.

THE CAMPUS BOARD

The campus board has been a popular tool since it was developed by top climber Wolfgang Güllich in the late 1980s. It consists of horizontal strips of wood attached to an overhung panel. To use the campus board, you move up the rungs of the board, alternating hands and skipping rungs to increase the difficulty of the training.

Campusing is good training for climbing in two ways. First, it dynamically overloads finger and elbow tendons, pushing past normal safeguard reflexes in muscles and allowing greater recruitment of other muscles to fire more of their fibers and pull together effectively. Second, it forces the climber to master the ability to move her body up with one hand doing most of the pulling, while the other pushes down, a helpful and powerful move to master when holds are poor or far apart. The stronger a climber is at dynamic one-arm pulling, the easier a given bouldering move is likely to feel.

Smart use of the campus board can enhance your climbing, but it has its limits. As Justen Sjong, coach at Movement Climbing and Fitness gym in Boulder, Colorado, says, "Campus board training alone will give you some gains, but ultimately you will end in a plateau. Each time a climber leaps forward with strengths, they must recalibrate their technique. A campus board won't teach you how to move. It only teaches you how to pull on a hold—almost always an edge—and to control the next hold."

A downside of campusing is that, without feet, the movements are too simple to match well with actual bouldering where, except occasionally on very steep overhangs, feet are always part of the equation. Furthermore, the campus board has huge potential for serious injury, especially to vulnerable elbows and fingers. Without ample rest, stretching, and working of antagonistic muscle groups, repeated campusing sessions are a sure road to ruin.

As with fingerboards, a thorough warm-up is essential. Don't campus after a bouldering session or when you are tired or not feeling at your best. Your primary focus should be on short, powerful bursts of movement with thorough recovery between sets. Vary the size of the rungs, use the open-hand grip whenever possible, and if any part of your body feels the least bit out of order, don't push it.

Build power using a campus board.

Related to the campus board but far less useful for bouldering is the Bachar ladder, a series of rungs strung on two parallel strands of rope, set at a fairly overhung angle. The climber ascends without using his feet, alternating rungs, much like a campus board. Neither the consistently large holds nor focus on stamina are particularly desirable for bouldering training. And as with campusing, misuse of this tool can lead to serious injury.

THE SYSTEM BOARD

The system board is essentially a small fairly overhung climbing wall with systematically arranged holds. Here the climber can select a type of hand movement to repeat and perfect, using either arm. You might want to improve your power at locking off a three-finger, one-pad edge. With a system board, you can set that exact move up, and practice it identically on either arm. You could hold it a few seconds, reverse it, do it again on the other hand, and repeat. The consistent eccentric and concentric muscle movements recruit whole muscle groups and foster muscle development of a type highly applicable to bouldering, an important benefit of any training regimen.

System training on a steep wall

The primary problem with the system board is (no pun intended) boredom. You must have a great deal of self-discipline to follow through on a repetitive program of limited moves. Making the most of these sessions also means keeping fairly close records of your workouts to see what is working and what is not, which can also be seen as a chore. If you are unwilling to track your progress so precisely, you may be better off focusing on training for power through actual bouldering.

CLIMBING WITH A WEIGHT BELT

A number of coaches and authors of training materials suggest climbing with a weight belt. The idea is that increased weight will force muscles to work harder through the moves and develop faster and better as a result. But climbing is a heavily technique-dependent sport and adding weight to actual climbing moves can alter and confuse the neural pathways established as you climb. The only way that I can see this tactic working is by confining this activity to simple movements like you would find on a system board and on generous holds.

Be careful: Added weight means greater loading on finger and elbow tendons. To avoid injury, be careful not to add too much weight. For bouldering training, there are better ways to use your time. Sport-specificity remains the crucial principle in all training situations, and climbing with weights of any kind works against what's needed for bouldering.

TRAINING FOR POWER THROUGH BOULDERING

Bouldering itself is one of the very best ways to train for power. Chuck Fryberger, a top boulderer and climbing filmmaker puts it this way: "If there's one thing that all the top climbers have in common, it's that they all spend an insane amount of time climbing." As those early climbers at Fontainebleau knew, bouldering develops power and technique and is one of the best ways to train for all types of climbing.

Yet using the act of bouldering as your primary training is potentially less efficient than pure strength training. For example, on any given bouldering day, a climber may do 100 or 200 moves, of which, after subtracting warm-ups and poor attempts, maybe 50 percent are of any real training value. Of the 50 percent remaining, a substantial number are holds or positions the climber already prefers and hence are within his comfort zone and of minimal value. So it may be, when all is said and done, that less than a quarter of the bouldering tried is of genuine training value, a poor return on invested time.

There is also the problem of favoring styles of problems and holds in your current comfort zone. Choosing what's easy will not help you get stronger.

The solution? For a significant portion of the session, deliberately challenge your own weaknesses, try new moves and problems set by other climbers, and keep the pace and intensity of the session high.

Training for power through bouldering requires discipline, focus, and the ability to objectively assess—and amend—the productivity of the session as it is in progress. Many of us prefer to have fun bouldering and save the training for another time. My recommendation is to blend the two outlooks: Have fun but work hard and challenge yourself often.

PROBLEM SETTING ON ARTIFICIAL WALLS

This topic is worthy of a book in its own right but it has great application in training. Bouldering on an artificial wall implies that you will be selecting certain holds and sequences in order to create artificial boulder problems to try. Most commercial gyms will have a large variety of problems envisioned and preset by route setters; that frees your time for climbing and training. You can also build your own home wall and set your own problems.

The most important part of route-setting is creating lines that offer variety of movement. You want to be imaginative in your use of holds to create interesting and challenging moves. It takes time, as well as a creative sense of what the body can and does do while climbing, to get a good feel for this. Experiment with different hold orientations and types and think about how the feet, not just hands, might be placed. Bring a number of climbers into the process so you don't defer to your own strengths and weaknesses.

Important considerations for route-setting are wall angle and hold selection. To set a route, make sure you select a good variety of well-designed holds that are reasonably friendly to fingers. Avoid sharp pockets or other features that isolate fingers one from the other and could lead to injury.

The best wall angle for bouldering training is somewhere around 30 degrees overhung. Less than that and you are not getting real strength training; more than that and you can end up with monkey hanging that limits technique.

ENDURANCE AND STAMINA

It might seem contradictory for a bouldering book to mention endurance, since most problems come in at under ten total moves. Yet endurance comes in many forms, including the ability to recover between attempts, to make multiple attempts in one session, and to climb multiple days at a time. So while it is true that boulder problems are rarely like sport routes with 100-plus feet (an average pitch or rope length) of steady, hard climbing; there is also no question that the need for overall physical endurance is important. In addition, there are plenty of problems that clock in at twenty or more moves, requiring a different set of strengths and skills.

Defining endurance in climbing has always been a difficult task as it is almost always linked with stamina. If power is the capacity to apply force quickly, stamina is the ability to do powerful moves repeatedly, up to around fifteen to twenty times, maintaining a certain threshold of maximum effort. Below this threshold, maybe around 50 percent of maximum effort, you might be able to repeat moves up to fifty times.

THE INTENSITY OF BOULDERING

Ben Moon has been at the leading edge of climbing since the mid-1980s, climbing the first 5.14c route, Hubble, *in 1990. He has long been a proponent of bouldering and disciplined training. His film on bouldering in the Peak District, titled "One Summer," was one of the earliest videos dedicated to bouldering.*

Bouldering is more intense than climbing routes. All the climbing is compressed into a shorter distance than it is when you are doing routes. You are doing the hardest thing you are capable of, really. I have always wanted to climb the hardest things I can, and bouldering is about difficulty. It's a very simple style of climbing. All you need is a pair of climbing shoes, a chalkbag, and maybe a crashpad. You don't need a partner. Though I like bouldering with other people, working on a hard boulder problem on my own in a nice environment is very important to me.

Doing certain problems has meant a lot to me. The sit-start to *Voyager* (V14) in the Peak District was important to me, in part because it's the hardest boulder problem I've ever done and it's right on my local crag. It's a classic gritstone line. I did the first ascent of *Black Lung* in Joe's Valley in a snowstorm when it looked like I wasn't going to do it.

I don't know how bouldering is going to develop. There are a lot of very strong climbers all over the world doing some very hard boulder problems. People are capable of doing many more hard moves in succession, even if the absolute difficulty of single moves doesn't rise substantially. You have to be disciplined, work hard, set yourself specific goals, and climb on as many different types of rock as possible if you want to get better.

Ben Moon

You can also think of this in terms of time. A powerful two-move problem might take approximately ten seconds to do while a ten-move problem will be closer to two minutes. A long endurance problem may take five or more minutes—and longer if there are rests.

TRAINING FOR ENDURANCE AND STAMINA

Training for endurance and stamina, like training for power, is both simple and complicated. A large part of the challenge is persuading your mind to accept the pain and discomfort that such effort entails over a longer period of time. One of the appealing aspects of bouldering is the absence of protracted effort and long periods of focused attention. Train to have energy in reserve even after a lot of expended effort.

The best way to train true endurance, which is defined in climbing as operating at a reasonably low level of difficulty, but continuously, for at least five minutes or more, usually around twenty-five moves, is to have a good climbing wall available with big enough holds that you can recover on really easy moves or good rests. Putting in repeated long laps of thirty to forty fairly easy moves with limited but substantial rest time between them will build resistance to the infamous "forearm *pump*" that shuts so many boulderers down. The key is not to include moves that present any difficulty or resistance. Pure, flowing continuous movement is what is needed. Once you can reach 400 to 600 moves per session at the desired level of difficulty you are pretty fit in terms of endurance.

For pure bouldering the utility of this kind of training is relatively limited but it can provide benefits including balancing muscle groups, improving technique, and improved general condition. Be wary of using traverses for this kind of conditioning, however, as traversing tends to work only forearms to the exclusion of other muscle groups. Outside, *linking* together lots of easy problems with no rests between them makes a great change of pace from the usual all-out effort of working hard problems only.

Stamina or resistance is more difficult to define and train for because it's hard to find the threshold between power and endurance. It is anaerobic, meaning you cannot recover on the route; this forces you essentially to sprint to the finish. To train for stamina, you want between ten and twenty moves at a difficulty that is very doable but does not flow easily move to move and does not allow any real recovery or rest position. To up the ante, minimize rests between laps, looking for roughly a 75–85 percent completion rate for the problem, and lower as you get near the end of a stamina session. You should be out of gas at the end of each attempt, having to dig deep on each move. The total number of moves in a session might be 200 to 300, max.

Training for bouldering stamina is draining and should be done sparingly with ample recovery time afterward. Lots of rest, eating well, and ample rehydration are needed to be able to climb well after a hard stamina session. Too much time spent at this kind of climbing can result in plateauing or burning out, canceling any benefit obtained.

CROSS-TRAINING

Investing substantial amounts of time in other activities is unlikely to directly improve your climbing. But there is no doubt that periodically doing other activities can benefit your climbing indirectly. A regular routine of light aerobic activity, such as thirty minutes of running or biking several times a week can help with recovery and general fitness. Running, particularly obstacle running such as on steep trails, improves coordination and balance and helps to strengthen feet, ankles, and knees. Trail running also combines nicely with an easy bouldering circuit to log both miles and vertical feet climbed. The combination makes a great break from relentless sessions focused on bouldering difficulty.

As for weight lifting or other forms of fitness training, it is a matter of preference. Climbers will rarely benefit from increased muscle mass because the crucial muscles for most hard moves are in the forearms. There are advantages to certain types of non-climbing training. The most obvious use is to build balanced strength in the antagonist muscles that oppose certain common climbing moves. These include the triceps, abdominal muscles, and extensors in the forearms. Pushing exercises, in particular push-ups, are very helpful in balancing out your muscle groups. Bodyweight exercises such as front levers (very difficult) or hanging knee raises (easier) work the core abdominal area very effectively.

For most climbers, serious weight training that induces substantial gains in muscle size may be ultimately counterproductive. The additional weight that such training adds creates an extra and unnecessary burden for hands and fingers.

RESTING

You do not get stronger by work alone; you must rest and rebuild to gain the benefits of working. This means taking time to recover between climbing sessions. Very few climbers continue to have productive efforts in climbing on the third day after two days of hard effort. It is possible to go longer if you climb more moderately, but at some point your body will go into deficit and need to rest and recuperate.

For most people, muscle repair after a hard bouldering session takes from forty-eight to seventy-two hours to be complete. Sheer will power can not compensate for physical exhaustion in a technical sport like climbing, so if you are tired the day after a hard session, you simply must rest.

Resting is necessary, especially at Hueco Tanks, Texas. (Photo by Shannon Forsman)

A good pattern to follow is at least one rest day for each day of hard climbing. One day of intense bouldering means one day off or two days on, two off. More than three days in a row of hard bouldering rarely pays dividends. If your muscles don't give up, your skin will wear out by the end of the second day anyway.

Rest days are an opportunity not just to relax physically but to relax mentally from problem-solving. Unwinding with a good book and a visit to a café might be a good idea. If you're on a climbing road trip, sightseeing is a great way to get to know different parts of the world. Take a walk or go for a run to flush out toxins and aid recovery. Eat well and drink lots of water.

Many climbers recommend longer breaks. Taking a week or two off from

DANIEL WOODS ON TRAINING

Daniel Woods is one of the most powerful climbers and competitors on the world scene. With V15 first ascents and World Cup victories, he is an expert on dealing with bouldering difficulties.

To become physically fit for a World Cup or other serious competition, you need loads of power endurance. There are some basic things you can do to increase fitness. Go into the gym and set circuits of twenty problems, graded from V9 to V11. Allow five minutes on each problem, give each one your best flash go and try to do every problem within five minutes. Do that circuit, rest, and then finish your session with easier circuit training, getting in at least 2000 moves on the wall.

Mental training for the stresses of competition is critical, especially the nonclimbing parts such as travel and other logistical aspects. You want to be comfortable maneuvering in airports, able to handle missing flights, even deal with getting food poisoning at your destination. If you're used to things going wrong and are able to stay positive, you are going to be strong in your mind and able to compete well. Overall you want to be able to climb well even when your body is in shutdown mode.

The process is the same in achieving your outdoor projects, whether it's double or single digit difficulty. With *The Game*, I analyzed the movements and went into the gym, because the gym's the best place to get stronger. For *The Game* my compression strength needed to go up so I set problems on the sixty-degree roof at CATS, the gym in Boulder on fat pinches with giant swing-outs. I did a lot of fitness training: one-arm pull-ups, finger pull-ups, one-arm openhanded deadhangs, and a ton of ab exercises and ring pushups. I knew that my body had to be in its ultimate shape to do this boulder problem. On a crimpy project such as *Jade*, I knew my strength to weight ratio had to be really high so I watched what I ate and kept my weight down. I trained only on really small crimps on forty-five-degree walls, setting simulators I thought were harder than *Jade* so I knew I could do the problem outside.

Video is some of the best homework you can do for climbing. Seeing how other people move on rock—how they figure out problems—and getting beta before you go to the destination; it's all a huge help. Half the battle in climbing is figuring out the movement. If you already have the moves in your head, even if it's from different climbers, you at least have an idea of how the climb is done. Even if you end up doing it completely differently, you have someplace to start from.

Climb with other serious, motivated climbers. Community is huge. When you see hard climbs go up it gives you motivation to try new testpieces and to create new ones of your own. If you are isolated from other climbers, your progression can stall more easily.

climbing helps you gain new perspectives on goals and self-assessment. Breaks can aid in preventing injuries and allow for greater motivation when you return to climbing. On rest days and longer breaks, some light activity is helpful for maintaining physical fitness and well-being.

FLEXIBILITY, STRETCHING, AND MUSCLE BALANCE

The truth is that climbing rarely demands extraordinary amounts of flexibility. Yet becoming a better boulderer can certainly be helped by increasing your flexibility, particularly in your hamstrings and hips, especially for heelhooking and rockovers. Stretching the flexors and extensors in your forearms will help maintain healthy tendons in your fingers and elbows. Lifting and stretching out your chest area counteracts the tendency of climbers to hunch and curl over. The climbing training manuals on the market all depict the typical recommended stretches for climbers. I recommend stretching

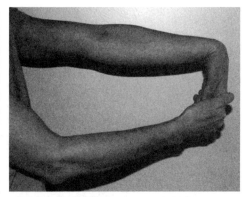

With the palm facing you, gently pull your fingers toward you.

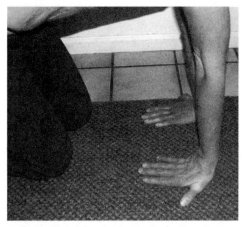

Pull your shoulders back gently, feeling the stretch in your wrists, forearms and fingers.

at most a few times a week, usually after a warm-up climbing session.

Muscle balance is perhaps a more important issue. Powerful bouldering tends to overemphasize back and forearm muscles. If allowed to develop at the expense of

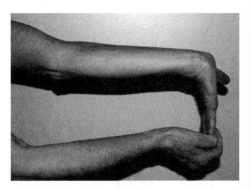

With the palm facing away from you, gently pull your fingers toward you.

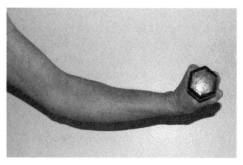

With a light load, lift the weight up and back toward you.

antagonistic muscles, the tension and forces these muscles produce can create serious problems including tendonitis of the elbow and shoulder pain. Pre-hab exercises such as push-ups, presses, and wrist curls, can make a huge difference in keeping overuse injuries at bay. Developing the triceps aids in locking off holds and pushing through long reaches. Seek out the exercises that work for you and invest at least an hour per week in maintaining healthy antagonistic muscle groups.

EATING AND SUPPLEMENTS

I firmly believe that the best form of body weight control is achieved through better technique. The more you can divert weight to your legs through your feet and abdominal core, the bigger the holds will feel. Slight adjustments can lighten that load by many pounds. Nevertheless, an optimal body weight for a climber is one that minimizes extraneous fat and maximizes lean muscle. Any unneeded body mass directly affects your ability to climb better.

It is easy to see diet as the key to climbing harder, but this is a big mistake. An athlete's body requires energy and nutrients to keep it functioning properly and recovering effectively. Your body is your engine for climbing; you need to supply it well. Eat whole foods, not highly processed junk food.

Weight control and maintenance is easier with high quality food. If you are training and climbing particularly hard, make sure you have plenty of protein to aid the recovery process. Just as important is a steady consumption of fresh fruits, vegetables, and water.

There is an ongoing debate about the role of performance-enhancing substances in sports. In endurance sports like cycling, some athletes' use of blood doping to promote extra red blood cells have ended their careers. In power sports, the use of anabolic steroids has cast a pall. Climbing is somewhat different. Neither steroid use (to promote muscle mass) nor blood doping (to increase endurance) improve climbing performance directly, so abuse hasn't been an issue.

Of the substances regarded as legal by official sports governing bodies, caffeine and creatine are the most likely to be used by climbers. Caffeine has been shown in a number of studies to allow higher energy output, though in some people it causes anxiety and nervousness, not good things in bouldering. It also acts as a diuretic, making attention to hydration a significant factor. Most athletes look at caffeine as no more stimulating than, say, regular sugar and no climbers consider it to be a serious issue.

Creatine (widely available as creatine monohydrate) is a more complex substance. It was first introduced in the 1990s to promote power and the capacity to apply force quickly. Creatine is a naturally occurring substance in the body and ingesting it promotes the creation of muscle mass. Inadequate muscle mass is rarely an issue for climbers, however, and the increased weight that creatine ingestion causes can be a problem, especially since the user cannot control which muscles are enlarged. Thus larger muscles such as the legs, the least useful for climbers relative to their size, add the most mass. Creatine must be taken with a great deal of water to be effective, and you can expect weight gains of two to three pounds in a given loading cycle. For most climbers this kind of gain is not a good thing.

MENTAL TRAINING

As important as training your body to move over rock is, it's not enough if your head isn't in the game. Don't neglect the mental side of climbing if you want to seriously improve your performance.

POSITIVE THINKING

Climbing with a positive outlook and positive companionship makes a huge difference in personal ability. Interaction with a circle of friends can boost spirits and improve technique. Friends provide motivation that gets you out to the gym on a night you might otherwise stay on the couch.

Keeping a positive outlook on the value and meaning of climbing in your life is also helpful. The physical and mental activity of climbing can make you a happier and better person and keep you going when you might otherwise want to quit. Taking pleasure in solving moves, meeting new people, or encountering new and beautiful problems and bouldering areas can motivate you to develop other areas of your life as well.

Pursuits and friends outside the sport should have value in your life as well, and not just if you get injured or can't climb hard anymore. They provide balance and insight into larger aspects of existence, aspects that make for a whole life as opposed to one lived in the narrow realm of climbing.

VISUALIZATION

Climbing is about actual movement and lived experience. Yet recent research suggests that the power of the mind in influencing outcomes in sports is substantial. For climbers, time spent thinking about and mentally visualizing, or rehearsing, the action of climbing a problem can improve their chances of succeeding on the route. Self-belief and confidence are boosted by this act of virtual climbing.

But visualization is not merely wishful thinking. It is a carefully thought-out strategy that can take considerable effort to do well. To practice visualization, you begin with an accurate mental portrayal of the problem and its environment. Every possible detail that you can remember about the rock and its surroundings makes the experience as real as possible and more effective.

Next, you visualize moving within this environment: recalling the approach, imagining the weather, and so on. Vividly re-creating every aspect of the moves on the problem, right down to specific micro-features and their feel on finger skin, takes supreme concentration. Finally, rehearse these moves, in as close to real time as possible, performing these moves successfully, while incorporating details like breathing, sequence-specific movement, and lines of sight. Repeatedly replay the sequence to ingrain the imagined ascent.

This is not a quick fix or a replacement for the hard work of actually trying the problem. Nor does it imply that visualizing will ensure a positive mental state. You have to be realistic about what you can actually picture yourself doing on rock. Some climbers get stressed out by this kind of mental exercise. But applied correctly, and in concert with physical training and hands-on climbing, visualization can boost confidence and minimize errors.

OTHER TOOLS

Sometimes you just have to step outside yourself and get a new perspective on your climbing. For that, you might want to consider video, a coach, or a climbing gym.

VIDEO
Digital video of others climbing is accessible as never before. Images that would have required bulky, expensive gear are now produced by cameras that easily fit in a pocket and cost a hundred dollars or so. Video is not just a medium for boosting egos; it is a

Chad Greedy films an attempt on **Let the Right One In** *(V14), Lincoln Lake, Colorado.*
(Photo by Caroline Treadway)

great way to look at how you move on and interact with the rock. Having a friend tape you on a problem may rapidly reveal some fundamental problems in technique that you can correct. Comparing your sequences with other climbers can help solve moves that still elude you.

Watching videos of climbers sending problems is a great way to prepare for climbing them, but it has drawbacks. Video often makes problems look much easier than they actually are since the flat screen can't convey complexities of movement, balance, grip position, and rock texture. A misleading visual picture based on video could be difficult to undo mentally and to overwrite with a more realistic take on the problem. Use videos as inspiration and general guides for sequences but not as a replacement for engaging with the real thing.

COACHES

In the contemporary climbing scene, coaching in bouldering is being accepted as never before. It really began to take off in Europe with the development of climbing as an organized sport. Coaches and trainers were employed to ensure that athletes were fit, reasonably injury-free, and well-prepared for the high stress and stakes of high-level competition.

Little by little, primarily in regional or national climbing centers, the idea of having a climbing coach has filtered out into the general population. This is especially true for the dozens of youth teams that have sprung up at local climbing gyms. Even adults hire personal trainers and coaches to

help them achieve a higher grade or master a certain climbing technique.

Whether coaching can help you as a climber depends first on the quality and abilities of the coach. Just because a climber has done some hard problems does not mean he is a good teacher. Does the coach have a really good understanding of the sport? Does he understand the biomechanics and training principles involved? How about an understanding of the mental game? Does the coach know how to explain these things to his athletes? Second, it depends on you. Do you really want to follow a coach's directions? Can you handle criticism? Can you be consistent in assessing your progress or lack thereof?

A good coach and the right mental approach to coaching will take you far. Yet if you want to get better as a climber, with a coach or without, you will have to be the final judge of what works. A coach can help with this process, no doubt, but cannot replace your own initiative and judgment.

CLIMBING GYMS

A good climbing gym is well-lit, well-padded, well-maintained, and clean. Any climbing gym worth its membership fees offers a variety of climbing training equipment, including free weights, workout machines, a campus board, hangboards, and so on, in addition to a good variety of climbing walls (see "Training Equipment" below).

Also check for supplemental classes and other offerings that indicate an active and vibrant scene at the gym, a factor crucial for motivation. There should be no superior attitude from the gym staff or other climbers. If staff are arrogant or you get a bad vibe from them, find a different gym.

TRAINING EQUIPMENT

Bouldering is a sport that requires little in the way of specialized equipment. But as described above, there are various devices that have been created to promote certain types of training, and if you climb regularly at a good gym, you will probably have access to them. Here I want to discuss some things to look for when selecting and using training equipment as well as some ideas for creating your own homemade versions of this equipment.

CLIMBING WALLS

Both at home and at the gym the most helpful training equipment you can use is a climbing wall. Even a very small wall can produce huge benefits if used correctly.

For variety and ease, commercial climbing gyms are the way to go, and here you should look for a good variety of walls with most of them set at 25 degrees overhung or more. Too many vertical slabs or horizontal roofs create poor climbing movement, as do inside corners and permanent holds (holds that cannot be periodically rearranged or reset). The holds should be updated and changed pretty regularly and the routes should provide a variety of techniques and hold styles.

A late night session at a home wall for Ty Landman (Photo by Jackie Hueftle)

You may want to consider building your own home wall as a supplement or alternative to outdoor climbing and gyms. I have access to thousands of problems on real rock within an hour of my house, as well as a number of excellent gyms in the city of Boulder. Yet a small wall in my cellar is a desirable training tool for me as well, not least because the demands of family and work make every minute precious. It also has the advantage of being easily tailored to my exact training or technique needs.

To build your home wall, you need only basic carpentry skills and tools. There are many sources, especially on the Internet, for suggestions on how to proceed. A simple wall overhung around 30 degrees going straight down to the floor is best. A few good footholds at the base can get you started on problems. Kickboards and other angles or features are mostly wasted space.

To outfit a small home wall, invest in a good variety of relatively small holds that are friendly to the hand and offer a wide range of gripping difficulty. Too many big, easy jugs and you won't gain strength. Too many small crimps and you can't warm up or have an easy day. Make sure you have a lot of smaller footholds as well.

Don't be afraid to invest heavily in holds; they are the reason you will want to climb. Metolius Climbing's website has an excellent guide to building a home climbing wall.

FINGERBOARD

Fingerboards train the number one weakness (or should we say number ten, for ten digits) for most climbers. Many hold manufacturers offer hangboards that feature multiple grip options including pockets and pinches. They are pretty pricey, however, and a better, inexpensive alternative is a homemade fingerboard: a simple set of wood strips, smooth and well sanded, which you can affix to a piece of plywood mounted above a door jamb or attach to a ceiling joist, as in a cellar. You can get the wood for next to nothing at a lumberyard or recycled materials store, often as scrap. Hardwood boards last longest, though softer wood such as pine will hold up for a while. Make sure the strips are solidly attached. One single-pad edge, about a foot or two long, and one half-pad edge should be sufficient. You can go smaller if you want, but be wary of the risk of finger joint injury.

The variety of fingerboard workouts proposed in training books and on various websites all boil down to building finger strength by hanging from one or two hands for roughly five seconds. Varying the grip position is a good idea, and shifting the number of fingers from four to three periodically helps target individual fingers more closely. Hanging from one or two fingers is a recipe for injury. When fingerboarding, always remember to warm up thoroughly.

CAMPUS BOARD

The campus board is a potentially valuable tool for developing power and finger strength. You want one with securely attached rungs made of sanded wood. Resin rungs made of rough plastic are too harsh on fingers for repetitive use. The board should be mounted about 3 feet away from any supporting wall or other features and set at an angle of 10 to 15 degrees past vertical. It should be at least 4 feet wide and 4 feet tall, and start at least 4 feet off the ground. Put ample padding at the base to protect the landing area, since the climber can fall suddenly.

Closely spaced rungs allow incremental gains in reach, important for training. The rungs should also offer choices between small and large holds, and incut and more sloping holds. In a commercial gym, campus boards can be quite large, but smaller home ones are often just as effective. If you have a home wall at 10 to 15 degrees, you can attach campus rungs directly, getting three tools in the space of one: climbing wall, system board, and campus board. You can also place "campusable" holds (holds that can be climbed without feet) at regular intervals. An excellent guide to building a home campus board can be found at the Metolius Climbing website.

SYSTEM BOARD

A system board is basically a compact climbing wall engaging feet and hands and is interchangeable with most small home walls. Its main advantage is that the holds are symmetrically arranged, allowing easy matching of holds and moves for both sides of the body. If you have a home wall with a sufficient density of holds, you should be able to easily match moves by small changes in hold position and type, mimicking the effect of the system board. For a home wall use a variety of hold placements to keep things interesting, while

maintaining a small set of symmetrical holds to use in system training if you want.

OTHER TRAINING EQUIPMENT

A few other items are handy for training. Among these are a small assortment of free weights, both dumbbells and barbell plates. Free weight exercises are great for maintaining antagonistic, or opposing, muscle groups. The actual weights you need are small (25 pounds or less), take up little storage space, and can improve strength to help avoid injury at little expense. Plates can be put on a bar for lifting or hung from a harness for finger workouts.

A grip exerciser is particularly useful for warming up the fingers and forearms on the long drive or hike in to the boulder field. These exercisers can take the form of putty, balls, and donuts; some are spring loaded. Some grip savers allow the climber to pull out against resistance, exercising the extensors and not just the flexors.

Along with these tools, you may want to invest a dollar or two in a notebook so that you can record the quality and content of your training sessions and plans for future workouts. Keeping tabs on performance is a great step toward real progress in climbing.

SAFETY

Essential to bouldering and training is developing an understanding of common climbing injuries and how to prevent them. You can avoid many injuries by using correct spotting and landing, taping against injury, and anticipating injury-prone moves. If you are injured while bouldering, there are strategies for recovery.

There is no question that compared to high-altitude alpinism or to free soloing without a rope, bouldering is among the safest of all types of climbing. You can easily confine yourself to challenges that take you no more than a few feet off the ground, as in traverses for example, or even choose to toprope a problem if you want. However, there is still ample room for danger in bouldering, especially if you are careless in your preparation for a problem or in your actual climbing of it. Furthermore, if you are a serious boulderer, the possibility of injuring yourself while training is ever present. A healthy boulderer is a successful boulder.

HAZARDS OF
BOULDERING OUTDOORS

Every fall in bouldering is a potential ground-fall, so your foremost thought should be, "What happens if I fall?" This is a question with ever-changing answers due to problem configuration and landing zone changes along the problem's length. Thus a boulder at the start might be a hazard at first, but maybe a steeply sloping bank below the topout presents the real challenge later on. Climbing safely means always planning ahead.

In traditional climbing, the climbing rope absorbs shock from a falling climber and dissipates that shock along many meters of relatively elastic nylon fibers. In bouldering, the body can also do a remarkable job of energy absorption, if you know how.

Recognize when to retreat and learn to downclimb. Being able to retreat from a dangerous position is safer than trusting everything to a fall on a pad. Sometimes climbing back down just a couple moves will make the fall doable onto the pad. Downclimbing involves careful thought, use of your eyes, and sense of balance. It is well worth practicing on a regular basis.

Another safety-related skill is learning how to climb carefully and deliberately in dangerous situations, when the objective risk of falling is great. The notorious *Whispers of Wisdom* in Rocky Mountain National Park has a steep, dynamic, and relatively safe lower portion which is the V10 crux. Above the crux section is a 25-foot-long, relatively easy, steep slab. Listen to the whispers: You don't want to fall from the top of this problem. Many choose to climb it in early summer when a large bank of snow eases the mind and helps cushion any fall. Others bail after getting over the crux lip. Gaining the mental wherewithal to stay cool on dangerous topouts comes from repeated bouldering on easy, tall problems. Keep out of trouble by knowing your mental and physical limits.

In falls, careful spotting and pad placement keep you safe, but so does learning how to fall appropriately. Most bad injuries in bouldering happen on impact with the ground, padded or unpadded. Keep a game plan in mind at every point in the problem. Ask yourself, "What happens if I fall here? Which direction am I bound to tumble? How can I best turn my landing into a roll?"

The best way to fall is to lead with the

feet and then collapse into a heap on your back or side into the pads, rolling if need be to dissipate the energy of the descent. Spotters can help by guiding your body into a safe location. Trying to remain upright is a mistake. It delivers the maximum force to your vertebrae and to vulnerable joints such as the ankles and knees. It's also unwise to blindly put out your arms and wrists to break a fall. Serious wrist fractures, elbow dislocations, and shoulder injuries may result from this instinctive reaction.

The most essential part of your body to protect is your head. Skull fractures and concussions can happen even in falls from low heights. Be particularly cautious about moves where your feet are level with your shoulders or head. If the problem is sufficiently serious, you may want to consider a helmet and/or a toprope. There are no hard and fast rules in this game, except that getting hurt falling is always a bad outcome.

Rarely is the boulder itself a hazard to the climber but there have been incidents where apparently solid sections of rock have shifted or fallen, injuring or killing climbers. Scope out your objective thoroughly, looking for any potential hazards, including boulders in the landing zone that might move, dead trees that might fall, etc. More typically, a hold breaks unexpectedly sending a climber on an out-of-control, violent fall. In this case, the only precaution to take is a thorough sounding out of the rock quality and hold stability. Do this with care. Sometimes apparently loose holds last for years, even decades, under constant use. In other cases, suspect flakes have broken under the maximal force exerted by a strong climber. My general rule of thumb is that if it flexes, it's going to break sooner rather than later. It's always better to deal with solid rock.

When bouldering, be aware that plants and wildlife can pose a problem; learn to recognize them and give them a wide berth. Poisonous snakes, such as rattlesnakes and coral snakes, are fond of sunning themselves on warm rocks, hiding in cracks and slots, or just showing up on the trail. Depending on the part of the country you are in, you may find yourself spending a lot of time in their habitat. Stinging insects are usually more of a nuisance than a danger, but anaphylactic shock is a potentially serious condition if you are allergic to bees or wasps. Poison ivy and oak also like to grow in rocky areas and can ruin an entire climbing trip. Large animals such as black bears or mountain lions are mostly reluctant to show themselves to humans, but use caution if bouldering alone after dusk. Learn how to avoid predators like these and what to do should you encounter them. A good resource is www.bearinfo.org.

A number of popular bouldering areas are remote from access roads and in difficult-to-navigate terrain. It is always wise to boulder with a small group of others rather than alone. Prepared boulderers learn navigation and compass skills as well as basic first aid. Take a cell phone in case you get in trouble. Leave your climbing itinerary with a friend or family member so someone knows when to expect you back.

Many more remote locations are talus fields in the high mountains, often above timberline. The hazards are different here than in the valleys or foothills. Dehydration and altitude sickness are real dangers if you are not acclimated. High elevations also increase the risk of bad sunburns and eyestrain. Especially in the mountains, the weather can turn quickly. Sudden thunderstorms bring deadly lightning, chilling rains and hail, and even snow out of season. Know how to take shelter from lightning, bring plenty of protective clothing layers, and remember that negotiating access routes, especially across talus, may be much more difficult when wet.

INJURIES FROM CLIMBING AND TRAINING

The dangers of bouldering at a reasonable level of difficulty are generally objective in nature. A degree of awareness and thoughtfulness will keep them well at bay. Moving up higher on the difficulty scale brings with it other problems intrinsic to the sport practiced at that level. Injuries from climbing are fairly common in high-end bouldering. It is rare to find a climber who has not hurt herself in the process of pushing the limits of her ability. That said, such injuries are not inevitable. Gain an understanding of how the problems occur and learn the best strategies for avoiding them.

The typical pattern of climbing injuries is one of overstressing a particular body part to a breaking point and being forced to take a break, then getting back into the game too early. At each point in this sequence there are opportunities to improve chances of avoiding injury and recovering faster from it, but only if you pay very close attention to the subtle signs you may be doing something wrong.

HOW INJURIES HAPPEN

Climbing is about moving a large physical mass, i.e., your body, using relatively small and potentially vulnerable body parts. When climbing is done correctly, you don't notice this basic truth as it can be masked by strength, good technique, balance, and sometimes plain luck. When the weight of your body is loaded poorly onto vulnerable joints, muscles, and tendons, however, trouble starts. The causes of this are basically two-fold: bad technique going into the move caused by inadequate training or planning, and trying moves that are dangerous regardless of technique.

An example of the former is attempting to lock off a small crimp at the end of a long day of bouldering. You are tired, underhydrated, and not moving as cleanly as you could. As you try the move, a poorly placed foot pops off a small edge, causing you to suddenly load your crimped fingers very hard with an eccentric force. If it's bad enough, you may actually hear a tendon pulley snap; other times you may feel a slight strain that allows you to continue climbing, continue to stress the tendon, and actually make a bad situation much worse. If you had backed off and come back to it rested and refreshed, the move and potential for protracted injury would have been trivial. If the pulley hadn't snapped but you felt something wrong, had stopped climbing and iced the affected region immediately, you might be up to speed in a week or two. Instead you could have a nagging injury lasting months, even years.

The worst is trying a move that isolates a body part and loads it excessively. The classic example is a one-finger pocket. No matter how strong or careful you may try to be, there is no way to guarantee you will not hurt yourself on a one-finger pocket hold. Another is doing a move that involves using a gaston hold high overhead or making a very long reach sideways. Both these positions involve a considerable risk to your shoulder joint, especially the rotator-cuff assembly. Yet another is latching onto a hold after a huge, feet-cutting dyno. The impact and subsequent swing are potentially very hazardous to shoulders, regardless of strength or technique. These kinds of moves can be anticipated and generally avoided, but occasionally you will want to do a problem that requires their use.

Often, the hardest injuries to avoid are not acute or sudden in nature but chronic ones induced by poor training habits, injuries not allowed to heal properly, and muscle imbalances. The training section includes some advice on how to train well and address issues such as muscle imbalance. The chronic injury is the most frustrating as it doesn't show signs of improving for long periods of time, long enough to prod climbers into counterproductive solutions, including drugs and surgery.

Avoid disaster with chronic injury by recognizing that the most commonly damaged tissues in climbing are often the slowest to heal. Tendons lack ample blood flow and restoring them to their normal state is a lengthy process. Also understand that healing requires, in most cases, the right degree of motion and stress to activate the healing process in a beneficial way. Too many climbers completely stop climbing during recovery and then resume the activity at too high a level.

Pushing through a serious injury is a bad idea, as it sets back the clock, forcing high levels of stress on tissue that is unable to handle it. It is important to carefully assess, alone or with a health-care provider, the extent of the injury and likely strategies for improvement.

Overuse begins when the microtraumas to tissues that are a normal part of training and strengthening shift into significant inflammation that can't heal without time, rest, and good nutrition. Healing also requires antagonistic muscle balance and maintaining a variety of activity.

PREPARATION: AVOIDING INJURY

To avoid climbing injuries, climb when well rested, always warm up, and stretch periodically. The first rule is never try individually hard moves when tired. This applies to training as well as in the field. For safe and healthy bouldering operate at your peak in the window between warm-up and fatigue, recognizing when you have peaked and adjusting your activity accordingly. During this window, stay hydrated and fueled to allow both better performance at the peak period and quicker recovery once you have quit for the day. Despite the stories of heroic sends on the fifth day and on the twentieth try, never climb to exhaustion. You are only teaching yourself to climb poorly when tired, a habit that is not easy to break. It also opens the window to injury on otherwise easy problems and moves, the type of climbing which is not worth the sacrifice of a climbing season.

Warming up works best on a sufficient amount of easy to moderate climbing or, if that isn't accessible, an adequate amount of exercise to get your heart and respiration rate up and your body temperature elevated a bit. A warm-up period of at least a half hour is good but an hour is better.

It is a good idea, after you have warmed up sufficiently, to pause and stretch the joints and muscles that the climbing ahead will test. Although bouldering rarely requires a high degree of flexibility, a flexible body is preferable to a rigid one. Stretching the flexors and extensors in your forearms, biceps and triceps in your upper arms, and hamstring in your legs helps you move well when on rock and also boosts your power and resistance to injury. After a few minutes spent stretching, climb some problems that are of an increasing level of difficulty for thirty to sixty minutes. This should prepare you for actually testing yourself on something difficult.

Fingers. Fingers are the weak link in many climbers' strength, so it is not surprising to hear that they are the most commonly injured parts of the body. Most bouldering finger injuries take the form of strained or partially torn annular pulleys, the rings of ligament tissue that hold finger tendons close to the bone. The extreme forces that are concentrated on finger tendons pull against these pulleys and can cause them to separate. If you have a finger injury that results in an audible snap and pain and weakness in the finger, cease climbing and seek medical evaluation immediately.

Finger injuries do heal but they take a long time to get back to full strength. The best way to avoid them is to know your limits, especially near the end of a session, and avoid potentially injurious holds. Repeatedly working a move that uses a sharp crimpy hold in the same position is begging for injury. Pushing past strains or aches in the fingers usually just makes things much worse. As with all the injuries discussed here, seek professional help for accurate diagnosis and remedy.

Wrists. Climbers put a lot of stress on these complex joints. The primary issue is carpal tunnel syndrome, an irritation of nerves in the carpal tunnel, a fairly narrow tunnel that channels the nerves to the hand, through the wrist. A major cause of this is excessive keyboard use, especially with the hands held in non-ergonomic positions. The repetitive motion and stresses associated with climbing movement can certainly aggravate it. The other major cause of injury to wrists is impact, catching a fall on your hands for example, causing a sprain or fracture. Both types of injury should be examined by a medical professional.

Elbows. Elbow tendonitis is another common injury and major source of aggravation for boulderers. Overloaded tissues combined with inadequate attention to muscle balance and stretching, inflames the epicondyles, the tendon attachments of the forearm flexors and extensors, on the inside and outside of the elbows.

As with any climbing injury, pushing through usually makes things much worse. Climbing poorly when tired, overdoing training routines on the campus board, and ignoring the need for stretching and muscle balance can trigger elbow tendonitis. The best ways to avoid and reverse it include exercising antagonistic muscle groups, varying your climbing routine and terrain, rest, and icing the affected areas. Seek medical advice for any case that persists or makes even moderate climbing impossible.

Shoulders. The human shoulder is a complicated structure allowing a wide range of motion and great strength when kept in good shape. Climbers frequently abuse this marvel of engineering, especially in bouldering, when long reaches on steep walls are initiated and stabilized by the shoulders. The range of shoulder injuries is wide, from outright tears and dislocations, injuries which are very painful and often require surgical repair, to chronic problems such as impingement and arthritis.

The shoulder is most vulnerable to injury when it is in an extended position such as a long reach to a hold, especially one that is off to one side. Any position where the shoulders are locked into a rigid position is a potentially serious problem but especially a dynamic one in which the climber's weight is swinging from one extended arm. These are the moves that can damage or tear tendons in the rotator-cuff assembly supporting the shoulder, possibly resulting in surgery and many months off.

Protecting the shoulder and preventing injury calls for regular stretching and rotator cuff exercises as well as careful attention to the implications of some kinds of dynos. Never train (on a finger board, for example) with a fully locked-out shoulder. Shoulders should be guarded carefully. A dislocation or subluxation (partial dislocation) can permanently weaken the shoulder.

TAPING

The use of athletic tape in climbing has a long history but it has primarily been used as a form of skin protection. For hand and finger jams in rough rock, tape gloves and layers of tape on the fingers are often recommended gear. Beginning with the era of modern sport climbing and bouldering in the 1990s, taping was used as a mode of reinforcing tendons, and today it is common to see climbers putting on tape for very crimpy problems or to reinforce injured fingers.

Various claims and counterclaims have been put forward regarding the scientific validity of taping against tendon injury. The consensus at this time seems to be that prophylactic taping against structural failure, such as an annular pulley injury, is marginally effective.

Taping injured areas can create a false sense of security that may lead to over-stressing them. I advise against using tape in this situation until you are clearly able to climb tape-free at a moderate or low level with no signs of pain or weakness. Using tape in the intermediate phase of recovery may help as long as you are very careful to not push your limits. Only when you are able to climb pain-free at a high level without tape should you consider your injury healed.

To apply tape effectively, a few basic principles are useful. After making sure that your finger is clean and dry, tear off the tape you will need. A typical piece will be about a half inch across and ten to fourteen inches long. A typical application is on the middle or ring finger to protect the A2 annular pulley below the first finger joint. Follow two snug wraps around the finger base with a wrap that heads up above the first joint. Make two wraps around this,

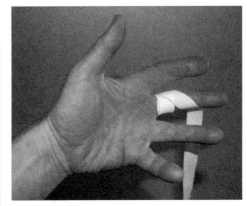

Step 2: Cross and begin a wrap above the first joint.

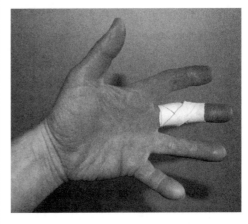

Step 3: Cross back and reinforce the first wrap.

then go back down below the first joint, forming a distinctive "X" across the inside of the first joint itself. Make one more wrap around the finger to secure the tape then tear off and responsibly discard any excess. This kind of taping is also very effective for finger pockets and finger jams.

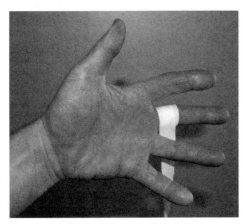

Step 1: A full wrap below the first joint

The tape job should be snug and moderately restrictive of motion without impeding circulation. A few bends with the finger and some warming up should loosen it a bit. If it becomes too loose, replace it with a fresh batch of tape. Be wary of relying on tape to support weak, healing fingers; respect the limits of taping in protecting your fingers. The best climbers are most often seen with little or no tape on their fingers.

LOWER BODY INJURIES

In bouldering, lower body injuries do not figure as prominently as upper body injuries, mostly because the stresses on the lower body are distributed across much larger masses of tissue. However, hamstring pulls and meniscus tears caused by bouldering moves can be quite serious and limit mobility considerably.

Lower body injuries in bouldering are usually the result of impact rather than overuse. Any impact injury that creates considerable pain and weakness in the affected limb or joint should be assessed by a medical professional immediately. Walking off an ankle sprain or knee injury can delay much-needed treatment, repair, and therapy. Cease climbing immediately and raise and ice the limb or joint.

SELF-MEDICATION

Climbers are notorious for pushing through pain, and one aspect of this is consuming anti-inflammatory drugs such as ibuprofen or aspirin to keep climbing. My principle on this is simple: If it hurts to the point of needing to take a drug to climb, you are doing something wrong. Treating the symptoms only exacerbates the cause. At most take a couple of aspirin to aid in reducing inflammation after a really hard session. More helpful is plenty of rest, good food, and lots of water to aid the body in healing microtraumas and eliminating waste.

SKIN INJURY AND CARE

In the big picture skin injuries are relatively superficial since they heal quickly with no aftereffects. But in the moment, they can have a major impact on climbing success. Careful attention to skin condition can be the key to sending that dream project.

Dry skin and physical trauma are both major problems for boulderers. Keeping your hands moist actually makes the skin stronger and more resistant to stress. This means drinking lots of water and applying a good moisturizer or climber-specific salve after climbing or using chalk. Keeping skin moist provides an environment where skin cells can rebuild as quickly as possible. Olive oil works well: It's cheap and it tastes good too. Do not apply moisturizers to skin before climbing or you may find the moves especially difficult.

One of the most insidious symptoms of excessively dry skin is the finger split, a separation of the finger skin, typically at the inside of a finger joint, which creates a small and amazingly painful slit in the skin that is aggravated every time you flex or open your finger. The best treatment for a split is to cover it with antibiotic salve and a bandage to promote healing. To climb with

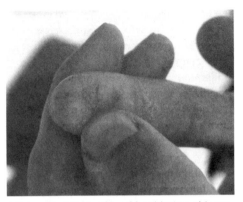

After a day or two of hard bouldering, this can happen. (Photo by Jackie Hueftle)

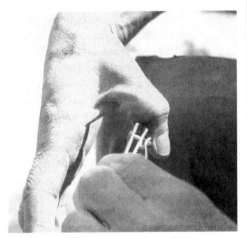

Painful but necessary: trimming a flapper (Photo by Jackie Hueftle)

a finger split, tape it tightly to keep it from opening more.

Similar to a finger split in some ways is the small incision caused by a sharp edge or crystal. Repeated tries can focus stress on a small area of skin causing it to erode and split. These are best prevented by close monitoring and taping as needed.

The classic show-stopping skin injury is the flapper. This is where the external layers of skin have been cut and peeled back by a sharp rock edge. They can bleed copiously and take several days to heal. Temporary fixes involving superglue and tape are extreme and they do not help actual healing begin. Flappers are best dealt with by snipping away the detached skin with clean nail or cuticle clippers as close to the live skin as possible. After cleaning the area well, apply antibacterial ointment to it and cover it with a relatively loose bandage, letting it heal for at least two days with no climbing. It is essential that the area be kept clean and free of debris and bacteria. By the third day, you should have regained enough skin to climb again with the wound area taped. In another day or two, it may be strong enough to be climbed on bare.

The best way to prevent flappers is consistent sanding of problem areas to eliminate excess callous buildup. Trim away small flaps of skin, which can tear into deeper flaps, as well. Close monitoring of your finger skin and knowing when to quit can mean a single rest day instead of four. As with tendon injuries, prevention includes careful climbing technique, such as not shock-loading your fingers by having a foot suddenly slip.

RECOVERING FROM INJURY

The adage "Time heals all wounds" is especially applicable to climbing injuries. Nothing else is as effective in healing even serious injuries. Once you have established the nature of the injury and its likely remedy, the hard work begins. Patience with the healing process may well be the most difficult aspect.

Regular icing and alternating hot and cold immersion in water reduces inflammation and promotes circulation. Getting a massage or having other bodywork done also can loosen up trouble spots and promote flexibility. Moderate use of anti-inflammatory drugs can help as well. Careful stretching and very light exercise of the injured area, provided no pain results, can be very beneficial. Doing other sports that involve cardiovascular fitness outdoors can keep you psyched about remaining active and focused on getting better.

The most important rule to follow is not to do anything that hurts the injured area, even a little bit. Testing it, when pain is involved, is always a bad idea, especially if you are thinking of how strong you were before the injury. Listening to your body and recalibrating expectations to match reality is an essential part of successful healing. Once you can do moderate moves with no pain, focus on low-intensity, high-volume climbing that promotes circulation and rapid recovery along with better technique. The worst injury is the one that doesn't teach you to climb better.

CHAPTER 6

Sasha DiGuilan and Matty Hong compete in the finals, ABS Nationals.

Competition

Competitions have been part of climbing for many decades, but they reached mainstream status only in the 1980s and 1990s. Originally they focused on roped-climbing events, such as onsighting and redpointing. After ill-fated experiments on chipped natural routes, competitions were held almost exclusively on artificial walls and holds, a development that changed the way we climb ever since.

While roped competitions in Europe remained relatively strong, in the United States they became almost extinct by the end of the 1990s, with the possible exception of junior events. What grew in popularity were bouldering competitions, usually held by local gyms. In conjunction with the rise of popularity in youth climbing teams, bouldering competitions became the new public face of the sport of climbing.

Men and women's bouldering competitions are seen usually in two basic categories, citizen-style and pro-style. The format of the citizen-style is relatively open and on the honor system. You register in a self-nominated category and try a number of problems, each of which has a point value. As you climb problems, you note how many tries it takes you to finish them, witnessed by an onlooker to verify your topped-out ascents. The atmosphere is typically crowded, festive, and fun. The stakes are low, with a raffle or other random distribution of gear and prizes to the crowd.

A pro-style comp is very different. Here the competitors are kept apart from the crowd and are required to work out a series of mandatory problems, usually within a strict time limit. Points are scored according to the progress gained on the problem, hold by hold, and judges make sure that rules are followed closely. Sometimes large amounts of money are at stake and the climbing level of the competitors is quite high. The public are spectators rather than participants. Competitions of this type are

A view of the competition walls at the World Cup in Vail, Colorado (Photo by Jackie Hueftle)

by invitation, or with a very small number of slots opened through a successful performance in a citizen comp from the day before or earlier the same day.

The tactics for success differ greatly between citizen-style and pro-style since the level of commitment required is very different. There are also basic similarities. The citizen-style comp can be good training for a pro-style competition if you are thinking of moving in that direction.

THE CITIZEN COMP: HOW TO SUCCEED

The first thing to do is plan ahead. If you want to perform your best, do not plan on bouldering all day and then coming into the gym ready to climb hard. Problems are most often set with big, powerful moves for the grade and will fatigue you quickly if you are not rested. Take at least one rest day before the event and try not to train too hard the week before. Make sure to register and pay in advance and arrive in plenty of time. This may save you a lot of time waiting in line. Make sure that you bring food and water as well. Some comps will offer sponsor-provided food but this may not be the best time or place to experiment so bring your own.

After getting in and picking up a scorecard, canvass the official problems, noting the most likely to get you the most points for your division. Let's say you have registered as an "advanced" level climber for a comp. This means you can probably warm up easily on the novice problems, do most of the intermediate ones first try and then get to the first three or four advanced ones without too much work. You will need to complete a set number of problems, usually around five or so, to be able to turn in your scorecard and have it counted. First, see if any of the elite problems are suitable for your size and style to make sure that you do not waste time on low advanced or even intermediate problems that are too hard. Make notes on the scorecard if you want, and ask around for other opinions about the difficulty or desirability of certain routes.

Having done a reconnaissance of the problems, the next step is warming up. Do this the same as you would for a regular session on the wall or outside. Fifteen or twenty minutes of relatively easy climbing should be sufficient and at the end of the warm-up, ticking off a couple of the harder problems in the division below your next chosen level is a sign you are ready to go.

Now you need to work on the problems in your division. Look carefully over the first four and select one or two that seem the most straightforward for the point value. If you are warmed up and well prepared, you should be able to get them reasonably quickly, maybe flashing or doing them in a few tries. You might consider a quick rest at this point. Next, look at the potential problems in the very top of your division or even in the next division up. Spend some time watching others work on the moves to better appraise the difficulty. Size up one or two that seem especially feasible and give them a solid try.

In the comp setting it is easy to miss obvious holds or sequences. The crowds, noise, and overall energy is distracting. Part of the game is keeping a level head in the middle of chaos. So before stepping off the floor, make sure you have noted all the possibilities and have a clear plan for what to do. Once on the problem, focus and do not hold back. If you can climb quickly and accurately the first time, you will not need to spend energy on a second try and can move to the next problem.

Making each try count means not jumping back on right away after an attempt. Physiologically, you will be less drained if you wait at least five minutes between tries. A slow and thorough warm-up between tries also speeds physical recovery. You can profitably spend the time watching others try the problem, sharing beta, and cheering your fellow competitors on to success. When your turn comes, take a deep breath and send it.

At some point the tap is going to run dry, no question about it. This is a crucial moment to weigh carefully the benefits of continuing or wrapping up for the night. Sometimes you may just need to take a long break and eat and drink something. Other times you are exhausted and should call it quits. Just as with a regular bouldering session, be aware that climbing when tired is a primary cause of injury. A popped tendon, a strained muscle, or an out-of-control fall is a typical result of trying too hard. It may be better to quit early and recover from the effort of the competition over a few days than to blow it and try to

A competitor cuts loose at the 2010 Vail World Cup. (Photo by Andy Mann)

recover from injuries that will take months or longer to heal.

Speaking of injury, be hyperaware of your surroundings in this kind of competition. The spectator crowds will be heavy and often oblivious to climbers above them. Keep an eye out for bad landing situations even as you climb. Having a partner to clear the deck is helpful as well. If you are worried about potentially bad falls and feel you need a good spot, it's best to come with someone you trust. The level of spotting ability in the average comp crowd is uneven at best. And remember to keep an eye out for wild falls above you as you walk near the walls. You do not want to be hit.

PRO-STYLE COMPETITIONS

Success in pro-style comps has a great deal to do with physical training. This kind of competition requires that you are able to quickly read or assess the route and climb from three to five fairly difficult and athletic problems in rapid succession. This means you must have a high degree of physical stamina and the ability to recover quickly between maximal efforts. You can obtain this only through a high degree of fairly specific training on similar boulder problems, which I will discuss in the next section.

You must learn the rules closely and

figure out the best way to acquire points. Not all competitions have the same format; understanding the rules may affect your result in unexpected ways. For example, how holds and problems are counted in relation to tries may change your score with unexpected and potentially welcome results.

You must find ways to build your mental fitness as well. Pro-style comps usually have spectator seating, video cameras, judges, and announcers. Some climbers wilt in the face of a watching crowd, while others feed off the spectators' enthusiasm. Keeping a level head and consistent effort going in the midst of the buzz of a big event is a skill you can develop. If you find this kind of setting appealing, prepare for it by training mentally for the situation as thoroughly as you can.

Having a settled routine is important on the day of the competition: Eat and sleep normally as much as possible, and stay well hydrated. Pack well in advance, making sure nothing crucial is missing. Gain as much knowledge as possible about the gym or site location in advance so that nothing will surprise you or put you off your focus on the actual event. Make sure you know where you should be and what time you should be there for all stages of the competition.

Pro comps typically begin by bringing the climbers out as a group to preview the problem for a few minutes before being put in isolation. Unlike citizen comps, in pro-style comps climbers cannot watch other climbers attempt the problems, so

you'll want to get what you can during the preview. Make quick mental notes of likely sequences and also observe what other climbers think about the problem. You will not have much time in a preview so try not to be distracted by spectators, announcers, or other competitors.

Before each comp, warm up as well as possible. Most venues provide a warm-up wall of some kind. Resist the urge to spend too much time here; focus instead on getting yourself ready. After warming up, take some time to stretch and relax a bit. Make sure you have brought warm clothes to avoid getting chilled while resting. When it's time to climb, have your shoes on and your chalkbag ready to go so that you don't waste time fiddling with gear. Once the problem is in sight, immediately begin re-reading it, first noting the likely hand sequence and finding the key feet. After you feel reasonably sure you understand the problem, take a deep breath, concentrate your energy, and climb it as well as you can. Often any nerves that may have been bugging you earlier will quickly dissipate as you actually concentrate on climbing hard.

If you top out, great! Jump down quickly and safely and try to recover as well as you can while getting ready to do the next problem. If the comp has an onsight format, you will not be allowed to view the problem outside of the allotted time limit so keep trying to de-pump and get psyched about the next step. If you don't finish it first try, try to quickly decipher the puzzle. When you are sure you know the answer, spend a little more time recovering before giving it everything once more. Remember that often in a comp, you will have no idea what anyone else has done. For all you know, nobody else got as far as you just did. Always try to climb your best, not worrying about the crowd, the noise, or the other climbers.

TRAINING FOR COMPETITIONS

As with other competitive sports, the key to doing well in a bouldering competition is doing a great deal of solid, preparatory training. Before you begin, remember that the single principle that all trainers and coaches agree upon, regardless of the sport, is to train as specifically for your chosen sport as possible. Training methods that do not have a close bearing on the actual activity may steal valuable time away from methods that do. So structure a substantial portion of your training for competition around the usual features of competition climbing: limited time overall, rapid succession of problems, need to make limited numbers of tries, minimal recovery time, and athletic style of climbing. Training that works within these factors will gain you the best results.

Preparing for a competition should reflect the need to achieve a certain level of effort and sustain it for a certain time. This may mean trying to do roughly twenty-five minutes of back-to-back boulder problems of between seven and twelve moves each, not at all like a typical two- or three-hour

session with practically unlimited tries. In a useful training session you want to make sure that you are hewing closely to the typical comp pattern of three to five problems with three to five minutes spent climbing on each.

Make sure that you are learning to read the problems as accurately as possible the first time and not wasting any time on false starts, misread sequences, and misunderstood holds. One example of reading would include studying as many different holds from as many companies as possible to understand the best way to use them. You want to try problems that are as diverse as possible, mastering all the typical techniques involved in comp-style problems.

Comp-style problems are problems that involve large sloping holds and features with long dynamic moves between them. They call for atypical body positions and a mastery of heel hooks, toe hooks, bicycle maneuvers, and compression. Comp problems rarely require good crimping strength or technical ability in comparison to more athletic factors such as power and stamina. The ability to make long reaches is almost always crucial regardless of overall style of the problem. Another aspect that is overlooked is dealing with height and falling from up high. Competition walls can be very high indeed. You want nothing to hold you back and having the skill to roll with a big fall is valuable indeed.

You want to be able to recover quickly after attempts, being able to time very precisely the moment when you can try again before your time clock runs out. This

Daniel Woods and Alex Puccio competing at the Battle of the Bubble in Boulder, Colorado
(Photo by Jackie Hueftle)

is an intuitive skill bred of a great deal of experience with this kind of event. Dealing with the mental pressure to climb within very specific time parameters is a hard-won skill for those who are used to a freer style of climbing.

To train for competition, spend the month prior to the event at a good gym with frequently changed routes, setting up your sessions to conform to the expected comp format. The elite competition level demands that participant boulderers do five very athletic problems from roughly V8 to V11 in a handful of tries each, at most, in about a half hour. These problems should be steep and reachy, with sloping holds and dynamic moves. You should be trying to flash every problem, focusing on quickly reading them as thoroughly as possible in advance and recovering quickly between tries. You should probably have at least a few of these kinds of sessions on busy days or nights at the gym, when the crowds and noise are most distracting. This will help you to deal with the pressures of the comp setting and format most effectively.

OUTDOOR COMPETITIONS

Outdoor competitions are very similar to citizen-style competitions. They are usually held at well-known locales with a high density of problems of all grades. Winners are chosen by a set number of completed problems. The main difference in rules is that it does not matter if you have done them before at some other point. While this would appear to give locals a huge advantage, many top-level climbers will travel to these comps and do very well even with limited knowledge.

For competing outdoors, weather and environmental conditions factor in. Depending on the place, you may encounter damp, humid weather or scorching hot sun. The Hueco Tanks Rock Rodeo offers dry desert air and sharp crimpers while the Triple Crown series in the Southeast is often damp and on big rounded slopers, as at Horse Pens 40. Natural rock can tear up your fingertips much faster than artificial holds at the gym, limiting the number of problems you can do in a day. The primary appeal for many participants in outdoor comps is socializing with hundreds of other climbers among the boulders.

Climbing competitions are different from other athletic events because the fields of play are each unique. Some competitions feature delicate, technical climbing, as in Europe for instance; while others, like those in the United States, lean toward displays of brute strength. Sloping holds and obscure sequences may be typical with one route setter, while another setter will focus on moves that turn climbers in unexpected directions. You never can tell until you get there. In the end, take heart in the fact that everybody at the competition is faced by the same problems as you. Prepare yourself as much as possible and be willing to learn from the experience.

CHAPTER 7

Thomasina Pidgeon and her daughter Cedar at Hueco Tanks (Photo by Jackie Hueftle)

Youth and Age

Bouldering is a popular and fun way to introduce young people to climbing. It is also a great activity for older people. As a youth coach, father, and a serious climber in my mid-forties, I have perspectives on both situations. Bouldering is a lifelong sport.

I first started to climb when I was about ten years old and have been climbing consistently ever since. One of the things that has inspired me to continue is the knowledge that climbing is an activity unaffected by most of the age-related issues that limit people in many other sports. I have seen the very young and the very old alike enjoying bouldering equally and would argue that perhaps of all the branches of climbing, bouldering may be the one you can practice the longest.

Bouldering builds on natural movement, like walking or crawling. Humans evolved to become very good climbers, and climbing is a form of movement that all ages can do easily, barring any serious physical condition. In fact, there are numerous examples of disabled climbers doing very well at the sport. Bouldering does not involve high-impact forces, fast running, or the sudden twisting so typical in many other sports and games, making it safe for young and old bodies. Intensity can easily be adjusted to suit individual taste or physical ability.

Climbing is uncompetitive by nature. Nobody has to keep score or referee the event. No teams need to be organized or games scheduled. There is no rule book to consult. You can climb when you feel like it, without a need for partners or spectators. The equipment required for bouldering is minimal: a pair of shoes, a chalkbag, and maybe a crashpad, which altogether costs a few hundred dollars and lasts a good long time.

Much like running, you can climb just about anywhere and anytime you want. With the advent of climbing gyms, daylight and good weather are not an issue. Nor is proximity to good natural boulders. You can find all kinds of opportunities to climb, from gym to boulder field, or you can build a wall in your own house for relatively little money and climb there. In other words, if you want to keep climbing your entire life, there is no reason to quit, ever.

BOULDERING FOR CHILDREN

I have often seen well-meaning parents, especially dads, who have been climbing awhile, try to introduce children to the sport by putting them on a toprope some-where outside, or even at the gym. Too often frustration results due to the complex-ity of the equipment, belay commands, and so on. Parents who are concerned with safety let this overshadow the actual climb-ing. This can be a turnoff for kids. This seems a shame, especially as any observa-tion of children at a playground or a back-yard shows that children love to climb. It's a natural and exciting form of movement that promotes imagination as well as exercise.

Few children feel comfortable right away with roped climbing. Fear of heights, lack of confidence in the equipment, and the unfamiliar nature of the activity turn many off right then and there, limiting enjoyment and skill acquisition from the onset. A more natural option is to take children boulder-ing, turn them loose on a climbing wall, be there to spot them, and see what happens. A low-hassle, commitment-free session on a well-padded wall may be the ticket to more enthusiasm for the game of climbing.

Brooke Raboutou on Mr Serious *(V8) in Hueco Tanks, spotted by mom, Robyn Erbesfield* (Photo by Andy Mann)

While I would argue that bouldering is a great way to introduce children to climbing, I want to caution parents to be extremely careful about doing the same thing outdoors unless the setting is safe and predictable. Outside, top-roped climbing is probably a better bet unless the parents are endlessly observant, have packed along several crashpads, and can spot well. When bouldering outside with children, plan ahead carefully and scope the terrain well. Loose holds, high falls, and misplaced curiosity can lead to accidents and injury.

Climbing is for all ages. (Photo by Andrew Burr)

RULES FOR CHILDREN

Even in the climbing gym, some important rules have to be stressed from the onset. First, the child must respect the needs of other gym visitors and stay out of their way. Second, the child must never wander or run beneath climbers on a wall. Third, the child must be kept from irreversible and dangerous situations such as climbing high above the floor. Fourth, the child must be taught how to fall safely so that even a relatively high fall can be managed safely.

Very young children may take some time to properly internalize these fundamental rules and should be closely watched at all times. Older children may learn quickly but should be supervised to some extent regardless. If you take a child climbing, you are ultimately responsible for everything and anything that happens, however silly or seriously it turns out.

TEACHING A CHILD HOW TO CLIMB

I have been a climbing instructor for many years and I've tried different methods of getting people to climb well, both younger and older. One thing I have learned is that shouting at people doesn't help them learn. Except in times of emergency, where you may have no alternative, shouting commands usually causes confusion and stress. Keeping an even and friendly tone of voice at all times helps get your message across; and a clear explanation and discussion of the route or problem prepares the student mentally to anticipate what's next, boosting his confidence.

Because climbing movement often comes naturally, let a child discover what works best for her according to how she feels. Climbing offers instant feedback to the climber, and children are fast learners. Resist the urge to explain technique or overuse climbing terminology. Instead encourage an open mind and curiosity about the puzzles that climbing presents. If the child thinks it might be fun to try to sit on a big hold, let him try it. It's a good way to think about balance. If the child wants to jump off the wall or swing from a hold, why not let them? Giving lots of commentary and directions, especially to kids under the age of eight or nine, generally bores and confuses them.

As you notice your child engaging with climbing moves, you may see better or worse techniques emerge. Focus on praising the good examples in a sincere way. Bad climbing techniques, such as scuffing feet, reaching too high, or poor body position, get ironed out quickly enough once the child begins to seek out more interesting and difficult challenges. If you want the child to reach to a certain hold or place a foot in a certain way, ask, "How about this foot here?" while touching the child's arm or leg that you want her to move. Actually placing or moving the foot or hand is counterproductive as it stifles the natural sense of movement so crucial to enjoying the game of climbing.

CLIMBING AS PLAY

Regardless of age, boulderers are players in a fascinating game. Children love to play.

They love to imagine and fantasize and dream. Feeding into this sense of questioning and curiosity is central to instilling a love of climbing. Bouldering is at heart a game that constantly asks, "What if?" Children love to try things out and see what happens. To whatever extent you can draw upon this, you build skills not just for climbing but for learning overall.

Examples of games include finding certain kinds and colors of holds. You can make up stories about them or have them talk to one another. You can hide small toys or treats at the top of a problem. For older kids you can have light-hearted competitions to find holds or problems or kinds of moves. Especially with younger children, resist the urge to structure and direct these games toward your idea of what climbing should be; what does the child think?

Children shouldn't be too closely directed in climbing until they have a better idea of who they are and why they like to climb. A child who climbs out of curiosity and discovery will be more likely to continue climbing later in life. They will also learn faster and become better climbers and enjoy the sport more.

EQUIPMENT

Another good reason to get kids into bouldering is the minimal equipment needed. Instead of rounding up a harness, shoes, and a helmet, you can start young children off scrambling around in nothing but bare feet or their regular shoes. A little chalk can offset the greasiness of gym holds, but it's not needed and a chalkbag is unnecessary.

If you are buying shoes for a young child, make sure you get comfortable, flexible slippers, not uncomfortable, tight shoes. If you live in a community rich in climbers, you may be able to find cheap or free second-hand shoes to get started.

Only as the child gets older and more serious about the sport should higher-end equipment be purchased, preferably with some investment of time and money from the older child. At this point getting good quality gear is essential, especially shoes. By the time the child is in his mid- to late-teens, shoe sizes should remain reasonably consistent. A good crashpad is a wise investment by this time as well.

CLIMBING CLASSES AND YOUTH TEAMS

With climbing entering the mainstream, more and more kids are beginning to climb with no experience within the family or circle of friends. Rather than letting them try the risky self-taught method, parents sign them up with the local gym for classes.

Climbing classes for kids can be a great experience. Introductory programs teach children the basics of the sport and tend to have a relatively loose structure. Kids will spend a lot of time climbing and acquiring skills and strength. They will probably not learn much about training or advanced climbing technique. The coach's role is to provide supervision and encouragement. The coaches and instructors tend to have fewer climbing skills and less experience compared with the team coaches.

Children who show ability and aptitude at the introductory level may be offered a slot on the gym's youth team or team climbing program. Parents should be apprised of what's involved. Some gyms will have several scales of teams, in order of climbing ability and age. Youth teams involve practice and training, and members are required to attend competitions that can happen year-round. Junior climbing teams will often have extra fees and other expenses. They may require uniforms, shoes, or other gear, which may be gotten for free or at a discount from a sponsor.

There is an extensive series of junior climber competitions in the United States, both in bouldering and in roped climbing, organized at the local, regional, and national levels, and even at a world level. Age-dependent rankings are determined by points earned in each event. Junior climbers who participate regularly in competitions may travel hundreds or even thousands of miles in a single season, depending on where they live. Teams may also be offered opportunities to travel to national or world-class climbing areas for a time, usually during school breaks. Teams are great opportunities for kids to develop their skills as climbers in a safe and supervised setting.

SELECTING A CLASS OR TEAM

If there is a climbing gym nearby, chances are that it offers youth classes and some kind of team. If you have a child who you think might be interested, briefly visit the class yourself before you bring the child. It gives you a chance to look over the facility,

Junior competitors cheer each other on at The Spot in Boulder. (Photo by Jackie Hueftle)

see the program in action, and maybe talk with the team coach and director without the distraction of a child along. If you get a good feeling about the class, suggest a visit to your child so he can try the class out. Most gyms offer first classes for free or a nominal fee. A good class has a ratio of one instructor to five or six kids or fewer and is focused on climbing, not nonclimbing, activities. Are the students enthusiastic, serious, and respectful or is the class too casual and aimless? What kind of tone is the instructor setting in interactions with students?

Make sure you understand the time commitments and expense required before enrolling your child in a class or team. Typically a class will meet once or twice a week while a team may meet three or more times a week. Ask if individual feedback is available for student progress on a regular basis,

if that is important to you. Find out what kind of equipment you will need and the best way to acquire it. Most important of all, sit down with your child and find out if this is really what he wants to do. Climbing is a great sport but it is not for everybody.

Climbing teams can offer great opportunities for young climbers, but there are also some drawbacks. The foremost is the emphasis on competition as a justification for climbing. On most teams, regardless of the sport, rewards and encouragement go most readily to those who compete well. Yet in climbing, there are numerous world-class climbers who find competing uncomfortable or tedious. Competition is not necessarily natural to climbing and to encourage children to see it as this is potentially a mistake. If a child chooses to drop out of climbing because of perceived failure at competition, something is wrong.

Usually junior comps are set for shorter folks! (Photo by Jackie Hueftle)

The emphasis should always be on kids having fun in climbing. That way, climbing is a natural, stress-relieving activity that becomes part of the child's lifestyle. If this approach is encouraged, children will still be interested in climbing even if you are not there all the time to direct them along. A sense of independence and responsibility is a great thing to foster in any child, and climbing is a great way to do it.

If your child is serious about bouldering and successful at it, whether in competition or bouldering outside, you should be careful to make sure that he keeps some sense of balance. There are a few examples of boulderers who have made a living of some kind as professional climbers, commonly through a combination of competition earnings and cash sponsorships. Such incomes are minimal, precarious, and rarely last more than a few years. The publicity and recognition given to top climbers is a huge lure to younger ones despite the relatively slim prospects and low financial rewards.

It's a good idea to seek out older climbers who can mentor your child and help her make good choices for the future. Point out potential role models who are both serious climbers and have good educations and careers. Make sure that bouldering is part of a balanced life so that your child will enjoy the sport for years to come.

BOULDERING AND THE OLDER CLIMBER

Our modern culture extols youth and the climbing subculture is no different. Every week, news of a hard problem done by a boulderer in his or her teens spreads quickly in the climbing community. But after climbers turn thirty they seem to become invisible. It's true that the pressures of career, family, and life in general may take their toll on time available for bouldering. Physical and mental energy are spread thin and motivation can slacken considerably. The climbing scene seems full of younger climbers who are coming at the sport and life from very different perspectives. Formerly constant companions also begin to drop out of the sport, limiting the number of peers you can connect with easily.

Yet there is no reason people need to fall away from climbing as they get older, especially not with bouldering. Aging is inevitable and should be accepted, but ceasing to do the things you love and that keep your body healthy is not a necessary part of it. There are a number of concrete steps to take right away to make bouldering better for you as you age.

JOIN A CLIMBING GYM, TODAY

Gym climbing is the most efficient way to maintain fitness in bouldering, and the social aspect and financial commitment will keep you there more consistently. Upgrade your gear, especially in the shoe department. I have heard many older climbers claim that their twenty-year-old shoes are just fine. Then they find that those board-lasted, loose-fitting, worn-out old beaters cannot stick to anything. Even changing your wardrobe a bit can help motivate you. Look at what other people are wearing and learn from them.

GET GOOD INSTRUCTION

If you are taking up the sport of bouldering later in life for the first time, get some good professional instruction and learn as much as you can about moving well and falling safely. Spend as much time as you can watching other good climbers and

John Sherman revisits his highball masterpiece, Germ Free Adolescence *(V5), Eldorado Canyon, Colorado* (Photo by Andy Mann)

emulating their climbing style and technique as you find what works best for you.

USE CRASHPADS

If you climb outside, get two crashpads and use them religiously. One crashpad is barely enough for relatively small boulders, and you may find yourself, owing to scheduling pressures, climbing alone a lot. You will feel much safer and more able to push your standard by having two or more pads to fall on. I regularly encounter older boulderers who started before pads even existed trying to boulder without them still. They rarely succeed, held back by the serious implications of injury from a fall. Old-school insinuations of cowardice or cheating associated with pad use are usually uttered by those who have quit the sport, often, ironically enough, because of injuries. Pad the problem well and your climbing level may rise a V grade or two instantly.

CHANGE YOUR ATTITUDE

The next step is one of attitude. You have to be determined to continue climbing and wanting to do the best you can with no excuses such as time or age or energy to hold you back. A regular climbing schedule, getting plenty of sleep, and eating well are essential. Warming up thoroughly and stretching are helpful for getting the most from your body. Not being intimidated by the scene at the boulders or the gym is also essential. Instead focus on learning from younger climbers, both in terms of technique and attitude. We are all just climbers at heart. Route setter and dedicated boulderer Jackie Hueftle says, "The longer I've bouldered, the more fun and more satisfying it's become. Every year I feel like I have a better understanding of a certain type of movement or strength or technique."

Too often I see older climbers looking wistfully at younger climbers, wishing for more strength and more time. Or they might reminisce about the good old days when they were young and strong. Focus on the present and maximize your experience in the here and now. Don't hang out with people who have negative attitudes, especially about aging. Keeping an open mind and remaining curious about bouldering is a good way to build confidence and energy.

While it is true that physical aging is a reality, bouldering well is not just a matter of physical effort. Nor in the end is it all about physical difficulty. John Gill has spoken often of his view that a boulder problem is not completed until it can be climbed with no apparent effort and as smoothly as possible. Focusing on making bouldering a kind of aesthetic process, more like tai chi or yoga, gives new meaning to the purpose of movement. Understanding deeply the relation between physical body and rock is no simple task, and it is certainly not reserved for the younger climber.

While many dismiss the idea of bouldering double-digits in their forties or beyond, it can be done. Superstar Ben Moon climbed V13 recently in his forties. I've climbed several V10s and V11s in my mid-forties. The key is finding time to train effectively, to rest well, and to take advantage of every chance you can to climb. The quest for getting better at bouldering in whatever way you want to define it never ends. Jason Kehl has said, "To be happy in bouldering you have to follow your own passion." May you have great adventures and find meaning in the journey.

Where to Boulder

Boulders are found everywhere on the planet, and every week it seems a new area is discovered with exciting and challenging problems. Still, some standout destinations have emerged in the past two decades that all serious boulderers must sample at some point. The places described below all have great appeal in terms of rock quality, number of problems, and setting. For most of them there are written guidebooks available and further information online that provide up-to-date changes in access, costs, and so on.

NORTH AMERICA

North America has no shortage of excellent bouldering, though much of it is confined to the mountainous edges of the continent. Most of the areas below are either in the mountain West or related to the Appalachian range in the East. That said, incredible bouldering opportunities are growing in the Midwest, especially in southern Illinois.

Dedicated boulderers follow the seasons from one area to the next, according to weather and taste. Others are fortunate enough to live in areas that are climbable year-round, such as Colorado's Front Range. The truth is that unless you live in the flattest landscapes of Florida or Kansas, the chances are there is decent bouldering somewhere nearby.

HUECO TANKS, TEXAS

Hueco is practically synonymous with American bouldering and for good reason. The rock quality and weather make it paradise for anyone seeking a great place to boulder, in winter especially. Hueco boasts more climbable, steeply overhung formations with excellent handholds than just about anywhere else in the world, especially for its size, with almost immediate

Jason Kehl, first ascent of To Die For *(V5),* Hueco Tanks (Photo by Andy Mann)

access from a flat road for many problems. Sharp crimpers and big slopers, arêtes, big grooves, *bucket* huecos: Hueco Tanks has it all in every grade.

With such quality comes immense popularity, and alone among the areas mentioned in this book, Hueco Tanks State Park and Historic Site requires reservations and guides to accompany climbers within much of the park. Visitors to Hueco are strongly advised to reserve spots for climbing as far in advance as possible for the days they plan on climbing there. During the popular times of the year, such as Christmas, there is a real possibility of not getting into the park without reservations. Matt Wilder's excellent guidebook, *Hueco Tanks: The Essential Guide*, gives the full rundown as does the website for the Hueco Rock Ranch at www.huecorockranch.com.

Once at Hueco, a few problems to try include *Sign of the Cross* (V3), *Fight or Flight* (V4), *Dragonfly* (V5), *See Spot Run* (V6), New Religion (V7), *Baby Face* (V7), *Better Eat Your Wheaties* (V8), *Choir Boys* (V9), *Full Service* (V10), *Diaphanous Sea* (V11/12), *Full Monty* (V12), and *Crown of Aragorn* (V13).

Once inside the park, you will find that a plethora of classics await from V0 to V15. Visitors are often wrecked after one or two days of bouldering here since the problems are steep and powerful on sharp holds that are hard on the hands. Plan to schedule at least one rest day for every day or two of climbing. And remember that Hueco is much more than just bouldering. In many ways it is the world capital of bouldering and a place where climbers of all nationalities and abilities congregate to sample some of the most amazing climbing on the planet.

The tall Hueco Tanks classic The Maiden *(V0), on East Mountain* (Photo by Caroline Treadway)

Getting there: Hueco Tanks State Park and Historic Site is located east of the city of El Paso, just north of the Mexican border and city of Juarez. It is readily accessible by air and by car. Visitors will find it most convenient to have a car to head into El Paso for food, supplies, and rest day activities.

Staying there: The Hueco Rock Ranch is a popular option, where you can connect with local guides and set up camp. Many climbers stay in motels in El Paso, which are fairly affordable and offer refuge from the long, cold nights of winter.

When to go: Hueco starts getting good in late October or November and stays good until roughly the middle of March. While the weather is usually crisp and dry with cool nights and daytime highs in the 50s or 60s F, cold snaps and even snowfall are not unheard of. Come prepared.

BISHOP, CALIFORNIA

Bishop is a collection of bouldering areas, all on public lands, near Bishop, California, on the east side of the Sierra Nevada range. The small town of Bishop is a friendly place to hang out, with the added attraction of hot springs and major ski/snowboard areas nearby.

Bishop climbing is world-class; it is the only area that rivals Hueco Tanks in numbers and quality of problems. Bishop's added attractions are hassle-free access to the boulders, amid an open and wild natural environment, and a wide range of rock types from granite at the Buttermilks to volcanic tuff at the Tablelands areas such as the Happy Boulders. There are also extensive, roped climbing options nearby, especially at Owens River Gorge. An excellent and comprehensive guidebook by Wills Young describes all of the bouldering areas near Bishop. See Young's blog at www.bishopbouldering.blogspot.com for updates on weather and bouldering news.

The climbing at the Buttermilks and other granite areas tends to be on fused, patina flakes that can shred the fingertips quickly, so bring tough skin. The area is also known for tall boulder problems. In fact some of the best known highball/solo problems such as Jason Kehl's *Evilution* and Kevin Jorgeson's *Ambrosia* are found within a few yards of each other at the Peabodys at Bishop. There are hundreds of high-quality, safer problems as well, in all grades. The most prized tick for the hard boulderer is the famous *Mandala*, first done by Chris Sharma, but there are many others, including *The Spectre* and *The Swarm*.

As with Hueco, Bishop is rich in classic challenges. At the Buttermilks, there are older tall problems like *High Plains Drifter* (V7) and *Saigon* (V7), and short intense ones like *Center Direct* (V10). But that is only the beginning. Outlying areas such the Beehive Area, the Pollen Grains, and the Bardini Boulders offer classic highballs like *Jedi Mind Tricks* (V4) and *Secrets of the Beehive* (V6), as well as short powerful problems like *The Maze of Death* (V12) and *The Spectre* (V13). New lines are going in all the time, especially on the terrifying, tall formations.

Though the problems are not as striking as those in the Buttermilks, the Tablelands feature many great lines. At the Sads,

Kevin Jorgeson taking a lap on the Bishop, California classic Mandala *(V12)* (Photo by Andy Mann)

Strength in Numbers (V6) is a standout, while at the Happys, lines such as *Morning Dove White* (V8), *Cholos* (V9), and *Toxic Avenger* (V9/10) await. There are so many excellent moderates in the Happy Boulders that it is superfluous to name them. For this reason, the Happys are usually quite crowded in winter.

The volcanic tuff canyons of the Happy and Sad Boulders provide fun, lower key climbing than the scary, thin highballs of the Buttermilks. Steep walls festooned with pockets and crimps are typical of the terrain found here. Usually much warmer than the Buttermilks, the Tablelands are a good option when snow lingers higher.

Bishop holds a lifetime's worth of climbing adventure, from V14 bouldering to alpine rock at 14,000–foot elevation. Every serious boulderer must climb at Bishop at least once in his lifetime.

Getting there: Most visitors drive to Bishop after flying in to big city destinations such as Reno, Las Vegas, or San Francisco. Once in Bishop, a vehicle is virtually mandatory to get around to the various boulder fields. It is worth mentioning that Wilson's Eastside Sports in Bishop rents crashpads, saving on airline fees and bulky baggage hassles; Wilson's also carries other climbing gear.

Staying there: Overnight accommodations range from The Pit, a cheap campground in an old gravel quarry on Bureau of Land Management (BLM) public land, to motels in town. Wills Young's guide has the specifics. You'll find plenty of good super-markets and restaurants in Bishop and, best of all, the world-famous Schat's Bakery to satisfy your sweet tooth.

Bishop's hot springs allow a relaxing soak in volcanically heated water. There are some free options, but be prepared for diverse companions. Ask around for the beta on these.

When to go: Bishop is best for boulder-ing late fall through spring, though snow is more likely here than at Hueco Tanks. When warmer temperatures arrive, a num-ber of higher elevation areas such as the Druid Stones offer cooler temperatures.

YOSEMITE, CALIFORNIA

It seems crazy to roped climbers that boulderers would travel to Yosemite to climb little rocks when 3000-foot walls are ten minutes from the road. Yet bouldering has a long tradition in the Valley, culminat-ing perhaps in the most famous boulder problem of all, *Midnight Lightning*, climbed in 1978. There are many blocks of excellent granite strewn through the park and even more in the high country of Tuolomne.

The climbing is on smooth, solid granite with edges, flakes, and slopers. Some prob-lems feature mantels and other relatively blank features. Many Valley problems are fairly tall and regarded as stout for the grade. Be prepared to work for your project and don't skimp on the pads. *Midnight Lightning* always attracts a lot of attention; but in recent years, a lot of exploration has taken place outside the Camp 4 area. Matt Wilder's *Yosemite Valley Bouldering* is the standard reference. While there is good bouldering in the sub-V4 range, most of the better problems are V6 and up. The Swan Slab Boulder is a good bet for moderate prob-lems. Standouts in the vicinity of Camp 4 include *Thriller* (V9), *The Force* (V9), and *The Dominator* (V12). More moderate problems include *Battle of the Bulge* (V6) in Camp 4 and *The King* (V7) in the Cathedral Boulders.

Getting there: Yosemite is one of the most popular and accessible national parks in the United States. Most visiting climbers fly first to San Francisco and drive east, but other options exist. You must pay a fee to enter the national park, either through a weekly or annual pass.

Staying there: Many climbers will stay at the famous Camp 4 campground, and for boulderers the location means excellent boulders right next to your tent, including

Midnight Lightning: the most famous chalk-mark in the world of bouldering (Photo by Jackie Hueftle)

Alex Puccio on the Yosemite classic V9 Thriller
(Photo by Jackie Hueftle)

the famous Columbia Boulder, home of *Midnight Lightning.* However, the crowds, stay limits, and other hassles of Camp 4 make camping at public and private campgrounds outside the Valley popular with many.

When to go: The best seasons for Yosemite are spring and fall. Summer is overcrowded and very hot on the Valley floor, and many climbers head for Tuolumne. Winter often brings huge snowstorms to the Sierra Nevada that prevent climbing for weeks at a time.

UTAH

Utah is packed with bouldering areas on all kinds of rock from bombproof granite to pocketed sandstone. Much like California and Colorado, there is so much rock in Utah that a lifetime spent climbing there would only scratch the surface. I will just touch upon Joe's Valley and Little Cottonwood Canyon, though many more areas exist to be explored and discovered.

Little Cottonwood Canyon is just minutes east of Salt Lake City, making it one of the most accessible bouldering areas in the country. LCC, as it is often called, is filled with fine-grained granite boulders that are usually very crimpy and feature stiff ratings. Be prepared to be humbled here.

Joe's Valley is farther south, about two hours drive from Salt Lake near the town of Orangeville. In a broad canyon lie thousands of beautiful black-striped sandstone boulders. Many of them are *choss* but the best rock here is as good as any in the world. Most approaches are relatively short.

A nice problem at Triassic in the heart of Utah (Photo by Andrew Burr)

Other destinations include Ibex, Triassic, Moab, Moe's Valley, and many other (some of them relatively secret) spots. The two bouldering guidebooks to the state cover this wealth of climbing well.

Consult the guidebooks for more, but in LCC, *The Twist* (V5), *Barfly* (V8), *Copperhead* (V10), and *Bully* (V11) are a few of the better known problems. At Joe's, classics such as *The Ramp* (V2), *Scary Monsters* (V6), *Big Boy* (V7), *The Wind Below* (V8), *They Call him Jordan* (V7), *Resident Evil* (V10), *Finger Hut* (V10), *Blackout* (V12), and *Black Lung* (V13) just begin to hint at the quality, with much more going in all the time, especially in the higher grades.

Getting there: The major bouldering centers in Utah are accessible by car from either Denver or Salt Lake City. Little Cottonwood is a short drive from SLC, Joe's a few hours. A car is essential.

Staying there: There are lots of accommodation choices around SLC, while Joe's offers mostly primitive camping on BLM land.

When to go: Fall and spring are best for both, though good winter days do turn up. The granite of LCC is notoriously slippery in warm conditions and Joe's is a hot desert in summer.

COLORADO

The state of Colorado is much like Utah and the rest of the intermountain West, absolutely loaded with boulders. From the crowded and action-packed scene on the Front Range to the quieter stashes of blocks on the Western Slope, there is almost no place in Colorado west of Denver that does not offer excellent bouldering. If you are traveling to Colorado to boulder, you will most likely visit the Front Range; but if you have time, areas outside the Front Range,

A beautiful alpine backdrop for Laura Griffith on Skyscraper (V5), Rocky Mountain National Park
(Photo by Andy Mann)

such as Newlin Creek, the San Luis Valley, and Durango, to name just a few, offer great unpublicized possibilities.

The Front Range of Colorado is the area concentrated between Denver and Fort Collins and includes low-lying sandstone and conglomerate areas such as Castlewood Canyon and Morrison in the south and Flagstaff Mountain and Horsetooth Reservoir in the north. Higher in elevation are foothill boulder fields such as Eldorado Canyon, the Flatirons, Boulder Canyon, Poudre Canyon, Arthur's Rock, or Big Elk Meadow. Areas at or above treeline include Mount Evans and Rocky Mountain National Park.

The concentration and variety of problems around Colorado's Front Range is probably unmatched in the country, and the weather for much of the year is excellent, allowing bouldering in all seasons, on both remote rock and roadside rock from VB to V15. For this reason many, many climbers move to the Front Range, especially the city of Boulder, to focus on climbing. It can be an intense scene: loved by many, hated by a few.

The classic problems are far too many to count or list. From the old-school problems set by Ament and Gill at Flagstaff and Horsetooth to the new-school desperates in Rocky Mountain National Park or Mount Evans, there is something for everyone in Colorado.

Getting there: The Front Range is served by a major international airport near Denver that is less than an hour's drive from most of the desirable bouldering sites. Two interstate highways allow easy driving access to and around the state. Having a car is very helpful.

Staying there: This is not as easy as it could be. The Front Range is crowded in prime tourist season and sometimes expensive. Camping around the city of Boulder is notoriously difficult and the best option is knowing someone there to stay with. Campgrounds serve Rocky Mountain National Park and Mount Evans.

When to go: Colorado offers year-round bouldering but most will want to visit in spring, summer, and fall. Summer is popular for the alpine areas in Rocky Mountain National Park and Mount Evans, which do not shed snow until mid-June. Beware of intense summer thundershowers, often accompanied by lightning. The foothills locations are choice in fall and spring though weather changes rapidly here, especially in spring, and snow showers are not uncommon.

OTHER AREAS IN THE WEST

Many good bouldering areas are found in California, including Joshua Tree, Black Mountain, and the Tramway. There are numerous unpublicized spots in California, Wyoming, and especially in the desert Southwest. The bouldering around Las Vegas, Nevada, is poised to become a major destination, and the bouldering in the vicinity of Leavenworth, Washington, is already recognized as classic. Ask around, call the local gym, or search the Internet: You will find helpful information posted by local climbers extolling new and exciting bouldering areas.

THE SOUTH

Over the past two decades, the southeastern United States has taken off as a major climbing destination. Aided in part by the high-profile outdoor competition series known as the Triple Crown, the southeastern scene has garnered rave reviews from visiting climbers and locals alike. The vast majority of the problems here are on excellent sandstone that forms clean, bold lines in all grades. There are amazing areas such as Horse Pens 40 in Alabama or Rocktown in Georgia, and much smaller local spots such as Dayton Falls or the Obed. Heading a bit farther west are the sandstone test pieces of Horseshoe Canyon Ranch in Arkansas.

The only significant drawback to the South is the climate. Brutally hot and humid in the summer, it can be quite reasonable in fall, winter, and spring, though pouring rain is an ever-present possibility. Despite the weather, the high quality of rock and boulder problems in the southern United States keep attracting visitors from around the country and even abroad.

Working a bit north you can visit the areas around Boone, North Carolina, as well as Rumbling Bald near Asheville. The bouldering around the New River Gorge of West Virginia is classic.

Getting there: The best place to begin a tour of the South is around Chattanooga, Tennessee, which boasts many quality boulder fields an hour or less away by car. Chattanooga is in southern Tennessee, not far from Atlanta, Georgia (a major airline hub), and close to I-75, making access relatively easy. The two primary destinations are

Christine Kornylak climbing Open It Up *(V0)*
at Stone Fort, Tennessee
(Photo by Andrew Kornylak)

Paul Robinson makes a huge reach on
Lost in the Hood *(V14), Cowell, Arkansas.*
(Photo by Caroline Treadway)

the Stone Fort in Tennessee (also known as Little Rock City), and Horse Pens 40 in Steele, Alabama. There are many other areas within a few hours' drive.

Andy Wellman and Adam Henry have published definitive guides to the *Stonefort Bouldering* and *Horse Pens 40 Bouldering*, respectively, which will point you to area classics.

Staying there: There are a number of campgrounds in the vicinity of each of the areas mentioned, as well as lodging around Chattanooga.

When to go: Locals seem to agree that November to March is prime season, though spring and fall are also good. In fact, bouldering is best here anytime but summer.

THE NORTHEAST

Bouldering is found everywhere in the Northeast. Especially prominent are the quartzite boulders and outcrops at the Shawangunks and the extensive granite boulders of Pawtuckaway State Park in New Hampshire. Other locales worth checking out include Lincoln Woods in Rhode Island and Smuggler's Notch in Vermont. Access-sensitive areas (where private landowners tolerate climbers if they stay low-profile) in western Massachusetts and Connecticut have devoted followings as well. For the ultimate urban fix, Central Park in New York City has problems up to V12 difficulty. The climbing is of all kinds, reflecting the variety of rock types and forms.

Bouldering in the Northeast has an old history but really began to take off in the mid- to late-1990s with the achievements of climber Dave Graham. His first ascents in New England remain coveted test pieces to this day. Many strong boulderers have picked up the torch since then, and secret spots still await discovery deep in the woods.

As in the Southeast, weather is the big limitation in this part of the country, though locals are famous for their willingness to endure difficult conditions. Summers are

Halcyon *(V11) is one of the finest problems in New England.* (Photo by Tim Kemple)

mostly hot and humid with epic flying and biting insects, while winters are usually bitter cold and snowy. Determination and luck make the difference here.

Getting there: None of the popular bouldering areas in the Northeast are more than a couple of hours from major airports; but be prepared for slow drives on winding roads to achieve your destinations. Guidebooks such as Tim Kemple's *New England Bouldering* or Ivan Greene's *Bouldering in the Shawangunks* are essential for finding the areas and problems.

Staying there: Campgrounds or local motels are your best bets.

When to go: Spring and fall are best, especially fall when the brilliant colors of the foliage electrify the environment.

CANADA

SQUAMISH, BRITISH COLUMBIA

About an hour north of Vancouver in British Columbia, Canada, is the beautiful granite bouldering area of Squamish. Huge blocks rest in lush old-growth forests below the soaring big walls of the Squamish Chief, providing a great playground for boulderers. The problems emphasize compression, heel-hooking, and slopers.

The weather is often wet, but that said, Squamish, due to its northern location, is an excellent summer destination when even high alpine areas in the United States are getting too warm.

Getting there: Squamish is roughly an hour's drive north from the metropolitan

Sheyna Button bouldering in the forest at Squamish, British Columbia in Canada (Photo by Andy Mann)

EUROPE AND THE UK

THE PEAK DISTRICT

While not known widely as a destination spot for bouldering, England's Peak District offers unique bouldering on a form of sandstone called gritstone. Short gritstone cliffs and boulders sit atop broad green valleys offering all kinds of holds and problems. This was one of the places that bouldering began as a sport, and climbers here continue to produce world-class problems at all grades. World-renowned climbers such as Ben Moon and Jerry Moffat set the standard, so expect grades to feel stiff. Within the limestone valleys are steep limestone cliffs that hold numerous hard, short sport climbs and challenging bouldering. Numerous pubs in the vicinity pour local brews that can ease the pain of a hard day's bouldering.

There are thousands of classic problems to choose from in the Peak. *The Rockfax Peak District Bouldering Guide* by Rupert Davies sorts it all out for you. The nearby city of Sheffield is the epicenter of British rock climbing and offers numerous indoor training options. This can be especially helpful owing to the frequent rains and generally humid climate.

Getting there: Flights to Manchester, England, are probably most convenient but Great Britain is relatively small, and you can be on gritstone within hours of arriving in London. Short and relatively flat approaches are typical for the Peak District.

Staying there: Campgrounds, hostels, and bed-and-breakfast establishments are in abundance.

city of Vancouver. Seattle is a few hours south. Access is easy to most of the bouldering. See Marc Bourdon's excellent guide, *Squamish Bouldering,* for the details.

Staying there: A number of local campgrounds in the vicinity serve climbers. Squamish has many other options including youth hostels and hotels.

When to go: Late-summer through fall, when it is both warm and dry, is regarded as the best time to visit. Squamish is low elevation and right near the ocean, so the climate is temperate. Spring and winter can work, too, but continuous rain and snow are possible at any time.

Gerhard Hörhager bouldering at Burbage West, Peak District, Great Britain

When to go: Fall is really the best time as the weather is most stable. Aficionados swear by winter for the best friction for bouldering, but the weather in winter can also change day to day.

FONTAINEBLEAU, FRANCE

Practically the world capital of bouldering, Font, as it is known internationally, has thousands of world-class boulder problems of every grade strewn through beautiful pine and oak forests, usually above flat, sandy landings. Move for move, there is no better bouldering area on the planet. It also happens to be less than an hour from the world-class cultural attractions of Paris and much more. Bouldering for its own sake was essentially invented here.

Font climbing can take some time to get used to. The rock is a fine-grained sandstone with a broad assortment of holds including the most sloping slopers ever seen on natural rock and the smallest, sharpest crimpers imaginable. Excellent footwork and a strong sense of humility are essential. Expect to drop down a whole number grade in ability as you get used to the rock. But the surroundings, the quality of the rock, and the subtle beauty of the moves on the problems will be ample consolation for most. With an area boasting close to 10,000 recorded problems, there really are too many classic problems to list. Consult the guidebooks, but climb whatever looks good; chances are it will be harder than it appears and classic.

Getting there: Fontainebleau is located about forty-five-minute drive south of Paris.

The forest of Fontainebleau is one of the finest bouldering locations in the world.
(Photo by Jackie Hueftle)

Roads run through the forest making it easy to connect different bouldering areas. Be prepared to spend some time getting oriented. A number of excellent guidebooks exist and http://bleau.info/ is a standard online source. Serious boulderers will want *7 + 8: 1789 Straight Ups in Fontainebleau* by Bart van Raaij, which only describes boulder problems from 7a to 8c.

Staying there: Overnight options including camping, gites (cabins for rent), bed-and-breakfasts, and luxury hotels in the town of Fontainebleau itself. The town is popular with walkers and tourists, too, and offers excellent services, so you have many choices for food.

When to go: Spring or fall are consistently good times for travelers to boulder here, but locals make the best of the area year-round. Conditions are best in winter for gripping the sloping holds on many problems.

SWITZERLAND

Thanks in large part to the efforts of climber Fred Nicole, in the mid-1990s, the small alpine country of Switzerland became known for more than just mountaineering. Today it is a major bouldering destination. In the Ticino valley in the south of the country near the Italian border, huge granite boulders nestle among small villages and orchards. Chironico and Cresciano have become world-renowned destinations as has the nearby Magic Wood. Many other smaller spots such as Brione and Fionnay add to the allure of the area. Access is sensitive in all these places owing to their popularity, small size, and proximity to local residents, so do your research before you go.

While Switzerland is often in the news for spectacular ascents of V13 and up, you'll find a good deal of excellent, moderate bouldering here, too.

Getting there: Flights to Zurich or Milan are your best bet and then car rental to get around. Guidebooks exist for these areas and information is widely available on the Internet.

Staying there: While there are camping options, the best time to climb here is fall and winter, making the local climber hostels a good bet. Switzerland is an expensive country for visitors, so be prepared.

When to go: In summer, bouldering here on the south side of the Alps is relatively warm, making late fall and early spring the most desirable times to climb.

Sticking the crux on Vecchio Leone *(V13), Brione, Switzerland* (Photo by Keith Bradbury)

OTHER AREAS IN EUROPE

Most of Europe has some form of bouldering nearby. New spots are discovered all the time in France, Spain, Italy, and Germany. Austria has incredible boulder fields and problems on all kinds of rock. The Frankenjura in southern Germany is well known for its short, powerful sport climbs, but it is also an important European bouldering center. Albarracin in Spain is a new sandstone area north of Valencia that has been described as comparable to Fontainebleau. Farther north, excellent boulders have been found in Sweden at Kjugekull, and Norway is simply covered with them.

THE WORLD

There are a number of bouldering destinations far from the typical European or North American climbing centers. These include Hampi in India and new boulder fields in Japan, Brazil, Bolivia, Chile, Australia, and South Africa. Only a few are described below for consideration if your budget and schedule allow it.

ROCKLANDS, SOUTH AFRICA

Rocklands in South Africa has become a very popular destination for the international scene. Miles of excellent sandstone outcrops and boulders carpet the terrain producing classic problems of all grades. The primary drawback for Americans is the high cost of a flight to South Africa.

The Cederberg Mountains are an extraordinarily beautiful location. The boulder problems at Rocklands are on all kinds of holds and surfaces from huge overhangs to thin vertical walls. Classics abound from VB to V15.

Getting there: Making your way to Rocklands involves a long flight to Cape

Paul Robinson on the spectacular roof of Shosholoza *(V12), Rocklands, South Africa* (Photo by Andy Mann)

Town, then a drive to the nearest town, Clanwilliam. The guidebook *Rocklands Bouldering* by Scott Noy will get you around the boulders.

Staying there: The website www.rock landsboulders.com has good information on camping and cottages for rent in the area and much more.

When to go: Rocklands is south of the equator meaning the prime season of winter is the Northern Hemisphere's summer. From May to October is the best time to visit.

AUSTRALIA

Australia is a vast and relatively unin-habited landscape. Bouldering has been developed in earnest in the past decade aided by visits from European powerhouses such as Klem Loskot and Fred Nicole. There are some very hard problems to be tried but also plenty of more moderate problems available at areas such as the Grampian Mountains north of Melbourne in Victoria Province. The bouldering in this region is on fantastically eroded sandstone similar to that in South Africa.

There are many other bouldering areas in this region of the world. Most famous is Castle Hill on New Zealand's South Island. Large, beautifully eroded white limestone boulders and outcroppings rise from a bare grassy hill offering thousands of problems in a spectacular setting.

Getting there: Visiting Grampians National Park involves a long, long plane trip to Melbourne and a fairly long drive west to the park. A car is mandatory. The

Topping out on The Fin *(V3), Castle Hill, New Zealand* (Photo by Brett Merlin)

guide by Chris Webb-Parsons and Dave Pearson, *Grampian Bouldering 2010*, should get you where you need to go.

Staying there: Numerous campsites and other possibilities including cabins and bed-and-breakfasts in the vicinity.

When to go: As with South Africa, May through October is best, though rain this time of year can be a problem.

Glossary

approach: The access route to a bouldering area.

assis: French for *sitting*. Used in Europe to describe sit-starts. Not to be confused with *bas*, which means low start.

back-slapper: A full-impact landing on your back, often result from swinging out, overcorrecting, and flipping in the air. The kind of fall you never want to take.

barn-door: An off-balance move may lead to your body rotating away from the rock if you lean away from the hold, so you swing like a barn door from the "hinge." Barn-dooring can result in a fall.

beta: Description of moves, holds, sequences, or other specialized information on a problem. Can also be extended to other areas of bouldering, such as access to areas, finding a campsite, etc.

bloc: French for the word *boulder*

boulder: Used sometimes as a synonym for a boulder problem as in, for example, "That boulder is graded V12."

bucket: *See* jug.

bulge: An overhanging portion of rock, often one that kicks back to a slab.

chalk bucket: A stationary, larger chalkbag that boulderers use for chalking up. Not carried on a problem.

chalk up: To apply chalk to one's hands. For many boulderers chalking up may take longer than doing the problem.

cheatstone: A small boulder placed at the bottom of a problem that allows a climber to reach the starting holds of a problem. Regarded by some as bypassing the natural challenge of the problem, cheatstones are more of a safety hazard than anything else as the climber may well land on the rock if she falls. Use a stack of pads instead.

chipping: Altering holds to make a problem easier, often by making holds larger or more incut. Considered unethical, bad form, and harmful to the rock. *See* gluing.

choss: Blocky, crumbly stone that breaks easily when bouldering.

cleaning: Removing extraneous matter from a problem such as dirt, vegetation, and choss.

conditions: Weather, humidity, or other environmental factors that affect bouldering.

contrived: *See* eliminate.

crimp: A small, sharp, incut edge. Also the mode of grabbing said hold, with knuckles raised and thumb closed over the forefinger.

crozzly, crozzler: A particularly uneven or textured edge or flake, often with the ability to remove skin.

crux: The hardest move or section on a problem or route. *See also* redpoint crux.

cryptic: Used to describe problems or sequences that are especially technical.

dab: To make inadvertent contact with something off-route while bouldering. This could include the ground, a pad, another climber, or an adjacent boulder. Dabbing invalidates the ascent in virtually all instances, though ultimately it is a judgment call by the climber. A dab in the middle of the crux is a bad thing, while inadvertently tapping a spotter while swinging on a good jug is not a big deal. It is a good idea to warn spotters in advance of moves where dabbing is likely so they can stay out of the way.

deck: To hit the ground violently. Also refers to the landing area.

drive-by: A crossover move done very quickly, often resulting in a swing that pulls the climber from the wall.

dyno: A dynamic move that requires a lot of speed and momentum to complete. Dynos could include completely detaching from all holds to complete the move.

ear: A positive and pointed flake.

eliminate: Any problem that relies on forbidding certain holds or feature that might otherwise be used. Sometimes, but rarely, eliminates are famous in their own right. Usually they are considered to be contrived.

Elvis leg: Uncontrollable shaking in the lower leg caused by fear and fatigue. Best prevented by relaxing and dropping your heels when standing on footholds.

erratic: A boulder that has been deposited by a glacier far from its source. Erratics are usually isolated and in unlikely spots.

exposed: High off the deck, potentially dangerous to fall from.

flapper: A detached flap of skin torn while bouldering.

flash: To do a problem first-try. *See* onsight.

Font: Short for Fontainebleau, the famous French bouldering area. Often used in reference to grades, as in "Font 7c," to avoid confusion with French roped climbing grades.

gaston: A hold reached overhead with a thumbs-down position, a kind of reversed sidepull.

Gill arrow: An almost invisible chalk arrow drawn by John Gill to show where he did a problem.

Gill start: Also known as a swing start. Linked with the great John Gill who started a number of problems by grabbing one hold, placing a foot, and springing with the other foot off the ground.

gluing: Reinforcing a hold with special epoxy so that it does not break. Usually it does anyway.

go again: A type of move done by grabbing an intermediate hold, then going again to another hold.

greasy: The most common complaint from boulderers about conditions. Greasy could refer to excess humidity, overchalked holds, or just having a high-gravity day.

groove: An indented feature in the boulder that is too big to be a flake but too narrow for a corner.

hand stacking: Placing one hand atop another to execute a move. Not to be confused with off-width usage.

headpointing: To do a very tall problem solo after working it out on toprope.

helicopter: A kind of fall where the climber rotates around a handhold, often quite wildly, before letting go. This can result in very dangerous landings.

highball: A problem that is very tall, at least 15 feet or more off the deck. The fear factor on a highball is dictated in large part by whether the crux is high or low.

hueco: A really large, deep pocket, named after Hueco Tanks where such holds are common.

intermediate: A kind of hold that is used to reset the body in a better position so that the same hand can quickly go again to another hold. Usually too small to use independently.

jib: A very small edge, usually a foothold, used mostly in gyms.

jug: A really good, incut hold.

jump start: To start by jumping to the first handholds. Can be a mandatory part of the problem, precluding use of cheatstones or pad-stacking.

link: To complete a route or a section of a route. *See also* on link.

linkage: Doing more than one move in a row. As in, "I am getting linkage on *The Automator* but can't do the crux on link."

link-up: To start on one problem and finish on another, usually by traversing into it. Link-ups are often given separate names and grades, as with sit-starts.

low start: Problems may have two or three different starts, depending on the stance or holds you begin from. A low start might involve crouching, but not actually sitting, to get to a set of holds below the stand-start. Many are tempted to transform sit-starts into low starts by pad-stacking.

lowball: A derogatory term referring to problems that focus on difficulty but never gain much height. Height often equals prestige in bouldering.

matching: The act of placing two hands on a hold to make a move.

method: A very specific way of doing a problem. A classic example is a big dyno instead of a technical, crimpy solution to a problem. Occasionally different grades and names are given to specific methods.

mono: A move that uses only one finger, typically in a pocket.

off-route: An adjective to denote anything not allowed on a problem. In regular roped climbing practice, this phrase implies getting lost; but in bouldering it implies that the object off-route is not to be used. Often used in defining eliminates.

on link: Trying to send. Sometimes used when someone seen climbing a problem tops out. "Was that on link?" you might ask, if they didn't seem too excited about it. "I just can't do that move on link" is a common complaint.

onsight: To do a problem first-try from the ground with no prior knowledge or beta about the line or the holds.

pad-stacking: Stacking pads to start a problem, work moves, or clean holds.

perch: Sitting high on a foothold to balance most of your weight on it, in order to be able to move a hand. Much like a rockover.

posse: A group of boulderers working on a problem together.

power-spot: To help someone work out a move by giving them a partial lift up. Not acceptable on an actual ascent.

problem: Routes on boulders. Because of the use of eliminates or different methods, problem can refer not just to a physical area of a boulder but a particular way of climbing it.

project: A problem that you have not done. A project usually takes a long time to complete, and is significant because of its grade or classic status. Also used for a problem that has never been done. Can also be used as a verb as in, "I am going to project *Nuthin But Sunshine* this summer."

projecting: Working a project or problem, often for months or years. Projecting can become an end in itself, occasionally with negative consequences.

pump: The state of fatigue in the forearms from a longer problem.

punt: To blow the last move on a problem or fail in some other heartbreaking fashion.

redpoint crux: The key section for success in linking a problem or route. May not be the hardest crux.

rockover: A move that relies on your lower body: you step high to a foothold and leverage yourself up until you can sit on your foot and then press up into a standing position. A rockover requires a strong sense of balance and flexible hips.

sandbag: A problem that looks much easier than it is or a problem with a traditionally very hard rating, as opposed to soft.

send: To complete a problem. The desired objective of projecting.

send train: The effect of one person sending a problem, which then motivates the rest of the posse to succeed.

session: A period of time spent bouldering, usually at the gym.

sit-start: Starting a boulder problem by sitting on the ground or on a pad. This is a popular way of increasing the length and difficulty of a problem. Derided by many as a sign of competiveness or hairsplitting, sit-starts often add to a boulder problem's appeal by creating a definitive start that is not as height-dependent as a stand-start. On a steeply overhung problem, a sit-start is very often the recognized start. A sit-start to an established problem is recognized with the acronym SDS or the suffix *assis*, French for sitting. In many

instances, it will have its own name and grade as well. *See* low start.

sketchy: Atypical, inadequate, or dangerous. Can be used for any aspect of bouldering.

slap: To dyno for and hit a hold, often with audible force.

slimper: A combination of the words sloper and crimp. Usually a narrow, sloping edge that cannot be grabbed using either open-hand or full crimp, but must be held with a frustrating combination of the two.

sloper: A hold that is not incut and often smooth as well.

soft: Used in reference to grades. Rarely are slash grades (e.g., V8/V9) popular in bouldering, so many will claim the higher option with the qualification of "soft."

split grip: To use separate fingers or finger pairs on different parts of a hold. Also known as Vulcan grip.

stance: A stopping place on a problem where a rest might be possible.

stand-start: To start a problem standing on the ground, usually with holds at head-level or whatever you can reach first. Stand-starts have been complicated by pad-stacking and cheatstones, so that certain problems have designated starts from specific holds as with the *Mandala* at Bishop or *Power of Silence* at Hueco. How you get to the start holds is irrelevant.

start: Where you begin a problem. Owing to the specific nature of bouldering, starts have become a source of debate. For example, a roof problem started with two hands in the roof and a foot hooked over the lip is very different from one started with both feet below the climber. Defining sit-starts, stand-starts, and low starts is a notoriously difficult proposition.

talus: Stones or boulders that have fallen or broken off from a cliff and are usually in a big jumble at the base. Often found in the high mountains, talus boulders can be the size of your fist or as big as a house. If big and stable enough, they are great for bouldering on, but they often feature terrible landings.

thumbcatch: Any small feature that you can grab with your thumb, adding to the usefulness of a hold.

tick: To send a problem. Or to make a chalked, directional mark such as a line to follow when doing a move.

tickmark: A white line usually made with chalk to designate a hold or the best part of a hold. Tickmarks should be removed after a session is done.

toe in: To really push in and down on your toe, typically on a steep wall, to get as much weight off your fingers and arms as possible and to extend your reach by pushing outward from your foot.

topout: The exit from a boulder problem to the top of a boulder. This can be easy or the actual crux of the problem: difficult slopers and nonexistent holds or easy but high and exposed climbing. Some problems lack topouts, simply ending at a convenient big hold at the end of the difficult climbing.

toprope: Climbing while tied into a rope secured above you. Most often seen in headpointing.

tracking: Using the same holds for feet and hands. Popular in the gym and occasionally found as part of an eliminate-style problem outdoors as well.

tufa: A long, snake-shaped feature that is usually pinched or liebacked. Common on some limestone formations, but seen on other rock types as well.

tweaky: Describes holds or even problems that pose a threat of injury to finger tendons. Tweaky holds are usually small, sharp crimps or pockets.

two-finger: A pocket that takes only two fingers.

work, working: Physically figuring out a problem. Working a project is the boulderer's most typical activity. It has nothing to do with real work.

Bibliography

Ament, Pat. *Master of Rock*. Mechanicsburg, PA: Stackpole Books, 1998.
Probably the first book dedicated entirely to bouldering. A revolutionary and profoundly influential book about John Gill. The first edition is a classic.

Eng, Ronald, ed. *Mountaineering: The Freedom of the Hills*, 8th ed. Seattle: The Mountaineers Books, 2010.
The Bible for climbing.

Goddard, Dale and Udo Neumann, *Performance Rock Climbing*. Mechanicsburg, PA: Stackpole Books, 1993.
A superb and still relevant guide to climbing performance

Hochholzer, Thomas and Volker Schoefl, *One Move Too Many*. Ebenhausen, Germany: Lochner Verlag, 2006.
The best book about climbing injuries available in English.

Hörst, Eric J. *Maximum Training*. Guilford, CT: Falcon Books, 2010.
A great guide to the mental game of climbing by one of the most prolific authors on climbing training.

____. *Training for Climbing*. Guilford, CT: Falcon Books, 2008.
A standard reference with all aspects of training covered.

Ilgner, Arno. *The Rock Warrior's Way*. La Vergne, TN: Desiderata Institute, 2006.
Another popular title on the mental game of climbing

Macleod, Dave. *9 out of 10 Climbers Make the Same Mistakes*. Ardlarach, Scotland: Rare Breed Productions, 2010.
An excellent book on getting better once you have advanced as a climber.

Sagar, Heather Reynolds. *Climbing Your Best*. Mechanicsburg, PA: Stackpole Books, 2001.
A good comprehensive look at climbing training.

Samet, Matt. *Climbing Dictionary*. Seattle: The Mountaineers Books, 2011.
More climbing lingo defined.

Sherman, John. *Stone Crusade*. Golden, CO: American Alpine Club Press, 1994
A combined history of and guide to American bouldering.

Soles, Clyde. *Climbing: Training for Peak Performance*, 2nd ed. Seattle: The Mountaineers Books, 2008.
Another good book on training.

Index

Page numbers in **boldface** indicate photos

About the Author

Peter Beal began climbing in the late
1970s, bouldering on the sea cliffs near
Portland, Maine. After a long stint of mostly
traditional climbing in New Hampshire,
he moved to Boulder and began a career
teaching art history while establishing hard
sport routes in the area. After the birth
of his daughter, he focused even more on
bouldering and writing about climbing,
which led to the writing of this book. He
hopes to keep bouldering seriously for
many years to come.

(Photo by Andrew Kornylak)

THE MOUNTAINEERS, founded in 1906, is a nonprofit outdoor activity and conservation organization whose mission is "to explore, study, preserve, and enjoy the natural beauty of the outdoors ... " Based in Seattle, Washington, it is now one of the largest such organizations in the United States, with seven branches throughout Washington State.

The Mountaineers sponsors both classes and year-round outdoor activities in the Pacific Northwest, which include hiking, mountain climbing, ski-touring, snowshoeing, bicycling, camping, canoeing and kayaking, nature study, sailing, and adventure travel. The Mountaineers' conservation division supports environmental causes through educational activities, sponsoring legislation, and presenting informational programs.

All activities are led by skilled, experienced volunteers, who are dedicated to promoting safe and responsible enjoyment and preservation of the outdoors.

If you would like to participate in these organized outdoor activities or programs, consider a membership in The Mountaineers. For information and an application, write or call The Mountaineers Program Center, 7700 Sand Point Way NE, Seattle, WA 98115-3996; phone 206-521-6001; visit www.mountaineers.org; or email clubmail@mountaineers.org.

The Mountaineers Books, an active, nonprofit publishing program of The Mountaineers, produces guidebooks, instructional texts, historical works, natural history guides, and works on environmental conservation. All books produced by The Mountaineers Books fulfill the mission of The Mountaineers. Visit www.mountaineersbooks.org to find details about all our titles and the latest author events, as well as videos, web clips, links, and more!

Send or call for our catalog of more than 500 outdoor titles:

 The Mountaineers Books
1001 SW Klickitat Way, Suite 201
Seattle, WA 98134
800-553-4453
mbooks@mountaineersbooks.org
www.mountaineersbooks.org

 The Mountaineers Books is proud to be a corporate sponsor of The Leave No Trace Center for Outdoor Ethics, whose mission is to promote and inspire responsible outdoor recreation through education, research, and partnerships. The Leave No Trace program is focused specifically on human-powered (nonmotorized) recreation.

Leave No Trace strives to educate visitors about the nature of their recreational impacts and offers techniques to prevent and minimize such impacts. Leave No Trace is best understood as an educational and ethical program, not as a set of rules and regulations.

For more information, visit www.lnt.org, or call 800-332-4100.